MW00811029

Escapology

COLIN MCALLISTER & JUSTIN RYAN

Escapology

MODERN CABINS, COTTAGES AND RETREATS

Figure.1

Vancouver / Berkeley

This book makes a lot of noise about a very tranquil subject: escape. It is dedicated to those who choose to leave the city in pursuit of a greater connection to nature and a quieter way of living, and to those who dream of following their example.

Copyright © 2020 by Colin McAllister and Justin Ryan

21 22 23 24 5 4 3 2

All rights are reserved and no part of this publication may be reproduced, stored in a retrieval system, or transmitted in any form or by any means, electronic, mechanic, photocopying, scanning, recording or otherwise, except as authorized with written permission by the publisher. Excerpts from this publication may be reproduced under licence from Access Copyright.

Cataloguing data are available from Library and Archives Canada
ISBN 978-1-77327-124-8 (hbk.)

Design by Jessica Sullivan
Authors photographs by Jeremy Kohm,
Great Canadian Cottages/Cottage Life

Editing by Michelle Meade
Copy editing by Melanie Little

Front cover photograph courtesy of The Backcountry Hut Company
Photo on page 1 by Anders Hviid-Haglund, page 2 by Suech and Beck.

Printed and bound in China by C&C Offset Printing Co., Ltd.
Distributed internationally by Publishers Group West

Figure 1 Publishing Inc.
Vancouver BC Canada
www.figure1publishing.com

Contents

Introduction

We're Colin and Justin, British interior designers, TV hosts and property speculators; cabin aficionados who divide our time between homes in Canada and in our beloved Scotland. During a twenty-five-year career thus far, we've presided over literally *hundreds* of properties. From Georgian townhouses in Scotland to latter-day mansions in North America, and from sky-high Canadian penthouses to mountain hideaways across Europe, it's been a fascinating journey. Recently, however, we've enjoyed a gentle change of direction, and now specialise in the creation of rural retreats, the unique nature of which inspired this, our fourth book.

Across the last decade, we've built, for ourselves, five family-sized cabins in rural Canada, a mix of joyful highs (oh, the pleasure of watching them come together) and stressful lows (cue timeline crisis, budgetary implosion and non-arrival of building materials). And whilst doing so, we've explored what it means to escape the "metropolitan" lifestyle, challenged, at every turn, by demanding topography and "extreme" weather patterns.

And do you know what? *Every* bit of stress involved in building these log homes, post-and-beam cabins and stick-built cottages has been worth it. We've fallen head over heels in love with the rustic idyll whilst carving a secondary life, far from the madding crowd of our regular urban existence. The ten-year stretch has bestowed upon us an ability to "pull focus" and decompress. Even as we write this book, we're working on several new cabin projects... and we relish the journeys ahead. More than ever before, we've now learned to take our feet off the gas, as and when schedules allow. You know: to improve emotional well-being and, indeed, physical prowess.

So why did we choose to write this book *now*? Well, in short because we wanted to share our experiences and inspire others to follow a similar path. The real estate market of late, particularly in North America, has been the subject of a steep, vertiginous ascent, and, accordingly, we've seen people struggle to buy property in their own cities. But it was here we saw an opportunity to help...

Along the way we've advised several clients to step back from their urban ambitions and direct reserves to the country. You know, buy something inexpensive, off-the-beaten track, fix it up, flip it and then bring the profit back to the city to supplement purchasing power. To us, that whole process is a no-brainer.

But aside from an ambition to encourage readers to dip their toes in the rural real estate market, we put this book together because we simply wanted to share with you a global cross-section of stunning retreats, each of which positively bursts with inspiration. Lost in our pages, we hope you'll be seduced by the escapist nature of the assembled retreats. Perhaps you'll feel driven to chase your own cabin dream, or be inspired to modify a regular urban or suburban residence, and thereby create the feeling of escape without so much as leaving the comfort of your own home.

We oft' opine that a cabin is like a clinic *and* a spa, both functions rolled up into one gloriously woodsy package. It's the very place unto which we escape to rest and recover. Little wonder, then, we feel so invigorated as we load out, after each break, and head back to the city.

As our appetite for the rustic idyll burgeons, we respect the landscape, all the time connecting architecture and cabin design (as sympathetically as possible) with the vagaries of the great outdoors. We've learned to master respites (for ourselves and our clients) that merge, due to the materials we choose and the finishes we select, into the landscape by which they're surrounded. That's why, for example, the Charles Gane–designed, post-and-beam beauty (page 137) works so well. Whilst undeniably commanding, it is tasteful and reserved, thereby complementing the surrounding landscape. It's all about fitting in and not taking over. We call this "architectural assimilation," and it's a pursuit that's become our (cabin-loving) holy grail.

This observed, our city lives are never far behind: much of our business operates against the urban sprawl, so we can't (and nor would we want to) let that wane. We credit our rural sidebar with providing the much-needed punctuation that restores our equilibrium. Isn't life all about balance? Emotional and social yin and yang? The necessity of warp with weft when it comes to weaving the fabric of our lives? In a nutshell, we believe that cabin time has a remarkably positive impact on our health, our well-being and our happiness.

And so, without further ado, welcome to a wonderful world of diversion. To a volume packed with inspirational homes, at all ends of the financial spectrum, the assembly of which we hope will enthuse and excite in equal measure. Some of the featured respites are starkly modern. Others are soothingly rustic. But they share one important aspect in common: they're all great escapes. Places where people can detach from the stresses and pressures of an ever faster-spinning world.

Sure this is a book for dreamers (who we hope will swoon over the featured cabins), but it's also a book for "doers," who we hope will find the narrative and imagery both compelling and insightful as they prepare to take the plunge into cabin ownership. Look upon *Escapology* as a compass—a navigation device, if you will—that carefully reveals "how" everything is done. From a rustic cottage nestled deep within a Nordic forest (page 69), to a robust mountain lodge in Montana (page 57), and from a breathtaking tree house in Canada (page 217), to a steel-walled, one-room "hotel" in Sweden (page 233), our featured abodes are all *strikingly* different. We hope our disparate library of cabins (and the wide and varied stories of their owners, designers and architects) may inspire you to dream of—and perhaps one day create—your very own fantasy retreat. But when it comes down to it, they proffer the chance to *escape*. And to live in harmony with nature, *far* from the madding crowd . . .

COLIN AND JUSTIN

Give Me Shelter

A rolling barn door slides to reveal an inviting bedroom: the ideal spot in which to tuck away from the world.

As much as the global cabin landscape is carved into multiple architectural styles, the aspects shared are the pursuit of sanctuary, the notion of escape and the delivery of comfort for everyone who visits.

But of course a huge variety of vacation respites exist—in an ideal world and when mastered carefully, each is a reflection of those by whom they're created or, indeed, occupied. At the end of the day, though, it's the fact they're all so different that we find utterly compelling.

In our extensive travels, we've seen many cabins, cottages, shacks and retreats (call them what you will), each serving to augment the profile of that which we consider the perfect respite.

ESCAPES OF ALL SHAPES AND SIZES

Log Cabins

Perennially popular, and oft' picture-perfect, but potentially dark if planned incorrectly. Historically, log cabins were constructed with small windows (to minimize heat loss and reduce weather penetration), so it's not unusual for them to seem a little on the dark side. In our experience, optimizing window scale has been a priority.

Undoubtedly, log cabins can be beautiful and, even if stricken by the aforementioned small windows, rebranded as "atmospheric" with a mix of clever layering, good lighting and illuminating textiles. Today, there's a renewed appetite for older building styles (and artisanal construction practices), so we're observing a higher frequency of log cabins being either restored or built from scratch. The good news: there are good deals to be had if you're planning to snap up an older structure. Whilst the appeal of log cabins is on the rise, the majority of buyers default to stick-built alternatives, perceiving them as easier renovation prospects.

If you can get your hands on an older cabin, one that's in relatively good shape, you could be onto a winner—because there's *growing* market appeal for updated spaces. But be cognizant that restoration can be more expensive, and that re-routing cables (or concealing pipework) is tricky, as it's more difficult to hide ducting and services when the cavities that are common in stick-built homes are absent. And of course be mindful that certain insurers run shy of offering standard coverage and terms. So do your pre-purchase homework to stay on the safer side of risk.

Post and Beam

Across many TV shows, magazine editorials and client projects, we've built, or reported upon, a plethora of post-and-beam structures (P&B), long since appraising them as an architectural style to which many cabin owners (and aspirants) are drawn. The visual nature of P&B construction, we suppose, and the marriage of intersecting beams and supports, is undeniably satisfying; intoxicating, even.

And with planning permissions and approvals, post-and-beam structures are easily adaptable at the building (and modification or extension) stage, because their visible "honesty" allows integrity to be more easily appraised than with homes whose "bones" are concealed behind acres of drywall and facing.

Modern Minimalist

As much as pursuing the rustic idyll is often a driving factor for those hoping to set up home (from home) in the forest or by the lake, it would be crazy to ignore the fact that, arriving in "cottage country," many folk sharpen their ambition and fall in love with the spirit of ultra-modern. For many, it's the contrast between organic backdrop and modern architecture that *so* appeals. One of our own clients, in fact, recently turned full circle on her remit: having originally aspired to a domicile with a rustic vibe, she eventually elected to pursue a modern minimalist route. Right-angled turns such as this make us remind clients how important it is to *properly* appraise ambition. To this end, we often suggest they rent a few places (in various styles) to get a feel for what they *really* want. The last thing we need is our clients to suffer buyer's remorse. Consequently, "Think twice, buy *once*" is our war cry...

A perfect example of modern minimalism is Vipp Shelter (page 233), an exactingly crafted vision of architectural restraint. We love the cabin's clean, precise lines and that it makes a massive statement whilst remaining modestly underplayed. A contradiction in terms? Absolutely not—sometimes our voices are loudest when we whisper, the strongest messages heard therein, *sotto voce*. Because less, of course, can be so much more.

Even the most basic cabin can be transformed into a contemporary retreat that shares the simple heart of the original structure. Updated, of course, to suit modern needs, as this before and after illustrates.

Scandinavian

"Scandi" is amongst our favourite decorative styles. An aesthetic birthed in the Nordic lands of Denmark, Sweden, Norway, Finland and Iceland during the early twentieth century by creatives in pursuit of simplicity and functionality, it grew in prominence by the 1950s. Whether layered internally as finishing detail (think white or off-white walls, acres of wood detailing, restrained shots of colour and black as a significant accent) or used as a dictum for exterior architectural vernacular (typically sleek clean lines, comfort and a connection to nature), it's a hugely popular directive in the "leisure home" sector.

Lately, as appetites for this simple yet commanding look burgeon, we've observed a turn towards jet-toned exteriors with cool wood detailing or, conversely, expanses of cool wood arranged with popping accents of black detail. Our own projects steer in this direction, favouring the simple lines that have made this vernacular so popular.

Mid-Century Modern

As we see it, there's a solid reason that mid-century modern has become so popular, particularly in the second-home community. In the 1970s and 1980s, a proliferation of cottages and cabins across North America echoed the feel of many Californian homes built in the 1950s and 1960s (Pan-Abodes and Viceroys being good examples). And as the leisure home sector has expanded, these properties have been snapped up by the style-conscious cognoscenti. Our own Plan B cottage (page 167) was radically transformed from its inauspicious origins as a wood-clad Viceroy-style cottage.

With sympathetic extensions and careful re-grooming to include a metal roof, replacement glazing and new siding, the cabin takes on an eminently more dramatic aesthetic, squeezed from its original "mid-mod" exterior.

Shabby Chic

For all we're committed modernists, we have a special place in our hearts for the whole shabby-chic frontier. If we're entirely honest, though, we've never been comfortable with the term itself—even though we get it.

Maybe we're hindered by the memory of the 1980s, when chic and shabby went hand in hand in *equal* measure. Back then it was all rough, white-painted wood and overstuffed sofas attired in clumsy, loose-fit covers. *Yawn.* We experienced so much of that aesthetic that, to be honest, we tired of it all pretty quickly.

These days, however, shabby chic has been successfully reinvented in a substantially woodsier, and far more eclectic, way than first time around. Cue a softer, less "shabby" look, with a much heavier emphasis on chic. It's way less twee, way less predictable, and *way* less boring.

Championing this new wave is Lynne Knowlton, one of North America's most in-demand stylists, whose captivating tree-house retreat features on page 217.

For us, the elevated home from home is playful, comfortable and indulgent in equal measure. Whilst old-school shabby chic was sometimes shambolic, its modern sibling—at Lynne's behest, certainly—has a running narrative that seamlessly links each element. It's all about upcycling, finding new hope for formerly cast-off items and assembling it all in one comfortable vision. Everything looks carefully chosen. Everything seems connected. And everything looks loved. *That's* the new face of shabby chic.

Carefully applied white paint unifies this rustic space, whilst providing a canvas that celebrates the structure's unpainted timber framework.

The list of styles goes on. Farmhouse style, for example, is also a fond pursuit of many of those who seek rural solace. As is nautical style, bohemian style and so on. There are benefits—and disadvantages—to all of the style categories. And of course, it all comes down to taste.

IS CABIN OWNERSHIP *REALLY* FOR YOU?

Sure, you've spent countless weekends at other folks' cabins, soaking up the fun with friends and family… and, goddammit, you've loved every minute. But are you looking at it all through rose-tinted spectacles? In the same way that in-laws and friends might love babysitting (but get to hand back the kids before diapers need changing), are you judging your suitability as cabin owners on the strength of a few stolen weekends? It's crucial to properly consider each angle of ownership before leaping into the metaphorical lake.

The first thing to consider is location. It's all very well thinking you want to be no more than 150 kilometres (93 miles) from your main home, but be warned: a "two-hour" drive can quickly turn into a five-hour marathon (especially in high season) if you pick an overly popular destination. It's all about balance, knowing the roads and assessing conditions during *every* season. There are so many districts from which to choose, so you need to do your homework. Potential cabin owners need to go out of their way to meet neighbours at their prospective new vacation home to ask about amenities and year-round road conditions. A call to the township may well reveal interesting history about the address being considered. There's *so* much to discover: building allowances for the property (is the building at its maximum size, or is there permitted scope to add rooms?), lake condition, which roads get snow-ploughed in the winter and just how life is during the colder period. Information is power—*don't* buy blind.

It's also worth considering smaller, "landlocked" lakes, which are often less expensive (as boaters have fewer places to go) than interlocking lake chains where travel and water sports are viable. Or how about a retreat somewhat away from (but still with access to) a large lake? Hmm? Taxes can be as much as 75 percent less. The mathematics of not actually being by water throws a whole new perspective on costings. You might find a huge dream cottage on a small lake for the price of a small cottage on a large lake.

Once you've set your budget, engage a realtor who understands your target area. Some realtors will have a widespread knowledge of one particular area, whereas others may be *au fait* with *many* areas... but masters of none. To make an informed purchase you need an expert: someone who knows the areas you think you like best but who is sufficiently clued-in to talk you through the highs and the lows of all options.

When buying any property (not least a holiday home), ancillary costs can quickly escalate, making that "bargain" deal less of a bargain than it initially appeared. Be informed about taxes, legal fees, insurances, property transfer costs and *much* more. Can you drink the lake water? Is there a well? No? Bad news: factor up to ten thousand dollars for digging before you can make a wish. Is your dream home from home on a flood plain? The bigger and more desirable the proposed water frontage, as previously described, the bigger the annual fees. If you went a little inland, those costs would lessen. A good realtor (in association with a reliable lawyer) will talk you through the salient issues.

Consider, too, how you might access your escape. Is the road in cared for by the local authority? If not, who maintains it when problems arise? And in winter? Who grits the icy surface? Is the cabin still accessible when the snow flies? If buying a house on a track that's not maintained by the township, at best you'll be sharing costs with neighbours, at worst you'll be paying a hundred percent of costs to keep the road passable when Mother Nature's icy fingers lock. And how about those bargain properties on an island? They sound idyllic, huh? But what happens when the water freezes and boat access is impossible? You walk? When is the ice strong enough to hold you? And what about that in-between period (sometimes a few weeks) when it's not solid enough to walk, but too icy for boat access? And let's not forget trying to get tradespeople to make that journey when developing or maintaining your, ahem, "dream" property.

Considering many cabins and cottages aren't used all year round, most will have ongoing issues of some variety that need to be planned for in advance. Matters such as opening the cabin or cottage ahead of season. Closing the cottage when the season is over. Maintenance, cleaning, security, seasonal requirements such as water draining and coping with fluctuating temperatures. Oh, and pest control. Be sure to take all of this into consideration.

By cantilevering the steel and timber walkway, the building appears to float above the softly undulating granite.

BUILDING FROM SCRATCH VERSUS A RENOVATION PROJECT

Unless you have patience, loads of cash and at least *some* relevant experience, a "from the ground up" project is likely to be tricky. You'll need to find land, arrange services (if your proposed plot doesn't already have them) and build a good relationship with planners. And besides: if that bargain plot seems too good to be true, it probably is. That which you consider a good deal is probably only cheap because of a million issues. Bottom of a steep hill? You'll struggle to get construction resources in. And in winter, you'll struggle to get your car up that hill when it's time to head home.

Ah, the joys of a fixer-upper. Feeling inspired? If you're looking to renovate a second home in a remote area, consider some of the challenges. That which is easy in the city or suburbs is likely to be far trickier in cottage country where there are fewer (often oversubscribed) tradespeople from which to choose. You're on the contractor–dating trail, chasing leads and asking everyone you meet for recommendations.

This low slung, timber-clad retreat glows like a beacon against the frozen tundra.

Deliveries may also be problematic and resources harder to handle. Don't be put off: it's still doable, but it'll take more time and money. You will also need to consider other factors such as who will let the builders in when you're not around, and what happens if they can't work weekends? Expect the worst and the best may surprise you.

THE MECHANICS OF ESCAPE

Many aging buildings and homes require excessive energy and water to run, factors which can dramatically contribute to the emission of greenhouse gases. If you'd like to assess your property's sustainability, discuss such matters with an architect or contractor, or seek out energy efficiency programs via your local government who, on some occasions, may provide rebates for going green.

Power—On or Off the Grid?

Most cabins and cottages (like regular homes) have centralized power, but some are off-grid, designed to be independent of public utilities such as water or electricity. As such, you may need to have services installed. Depending where the cottage is, and depending how difficult it is to access, this can run into tens of thousands of dollars.

Alternatively, you could install a generator, but these also need an oil supply. An average generator for a medium-sized cottage will skin you between seven and ten thousand dollars. And the oil supply can cost several hundred dollars a month. Some cabins may have log-burning stoves, central heating or baseboard heaters, but of course with all these services come maintenance and upkeep issues.

Septic System

Unlike city or suburban homes, most cottages don't have central sewerage systems. As such, many are serviced by private septic tanks. These have a shelf life of approximately twenty-five years, so if you're buying a cottage with an older septic, chances are there'll be a bill for $12K somewhere down the line for a replacement. And be warned: you can't just plonk a septic wherever you fancy: you'll need plans, warrants and sufficient property.

Winterized versus Non-Winterized

Whilst filming *Cabin Pressure*, we purchased a cottage which was purported to be fully winterized. An initial walk-through seemed to corroborate this but, being that the "slanty shanty" was a fixer-upper (and we anticipated big repairs regardless of what our report might find), we decided to save a couple of thousand bucks in fees by buying "as seen." Big mistake. Turns out our diamond in the rough was short on insulation, had been built with inferior boards and was about as hermetically sealed against the elements as an old barn. But hey: we lived. And we learned. And paid the best part of twenty thousand dollars to sort insulation and wiring so our cabin by the lake could become energy-efficient and warm.

DESIGN YOUR SPACE

The more carefully you plan your vacation home, the more familiar it will feel. But don't rush into the design only to regret your early endeavours. It's far better to strategize your objectives and then work through your list in as logical and timely a manner as budgets allow.

Wood, Wood and More Wood

By all means lavish your vacation home with a forest of timber finishes to add warmth and calm, but avoid the "matchy-matchy" approach of old, where your oak floor had to match your oak doors. Enjoy a sense of freedom and be inspired by the greatest designer of all—Mother Nature, she who mixes many trees in a forest to commanding effect.

Lighting the Way

Sensitive, well-planned lighting is crucial to help balance mood and create the ideal escape. For starters, ensure a generous spread of table and floor lamps that can be moved from zone to zone to satisfy changing daily requirements. And take a tip: in today's cabins, the humble dimmer switch is your best friend so that lighting levels can be moderated to create an intimate feel. Consider individual wall-mounted dimmers, as well as cable switch-controlled dimmers for table and floor lamps. And there's a bonus: with lower lighting comes lower hydro bills...

For those brave enough to recolour a traditional log cabin, the payoff can be spectacular. The trick, here, was to balance painted surfaces with darker elements such as timber flooring, leather-topped bar stools and contrasting kitchen cabinetry.

A roaring fire provides a warm welcome in this updated log cabin: a lesson in texture courtesy of stone, wood, metal and linen.

Furniture

Most people choose the furniture in their principal homes to be stylish *and* sufficiently well constructed so as to cope with the rough and tumble of daily life. But take it from us: furniture in the cabin context needs to be extra resilient, as it will endure *so* much more. In days gone by, it used to be the only furniture that made it to the cabin was the stuff deemed no longer appropriate at home. But these days, vacation retreats have become eminently more stylish than before; reflections of their owners, rather than little more than an assembly of discard.

Textiles

Feel your way to happiness by choosing textiles that are warm and inviting in terms of colour and texture. The feel-good factor is paramount and, just as you might layer on a lamb's-wool or cashmere scarf, so too can you drape your sofa, bed or dining chairs with throws and blankets to keep the chills at bay. Think "seasonal adjustment" and choose soft layers that can be piled on, or pulled away, as required. And don't be shy of thrift-store bargains: "previously loved" makes a lot of sense due to the transient nature of the vacation-home landscape. Local thrift stores are often packed with bounty.

Flames of Love

Man's relationship with fire dates back to the dawn of time and, to this day, there's no better way to create comfort and protection than with roaring flames. The hearth, after all, is the focal point of a winter room, a gathering place to drink whisky and share stories, and a welcome spot to blast the cold from your bones until your cheeks turn red. If you don't have a real fire, consider a twenty-first-century equivalent: a flickering hearth beamed through a wall-mounted flat-screen TV, or an electric-steam "flame" fire to provide the kinetic "heat" required to amplify the cozy quotient.

Olfactory Escapes

Candles provide gentle flickering light that feels romantic, escapist and cosseting. Scented candles are our biggest allies, a personal indulgence and a luxury to which we regularly treat ourselves.

HOW TO DESIGN A CABIN ON A BUDGET

Retreats and cabins should be relaxing, escapist worlds that tempt ultimate decompression. But if your haven misses the mark, don't despair: there exists an arsenal of low-cost fixes, employable to bring out the best in your sanctuary. The golden rule, though, is to spend first on maintenance and on your building's structure—so your cabin remains windproof and water-tight—before splashing out on a more superficial roster of surface items.

To fail to plan is to plan to fail. Focus ambition, manage your budget and *stick* to it.

PAINT

Painting is relatively inexpensive and, tackled properly, will elicit maximum results for minimum effort. But slow down: adept preparation costs nothing (only time) and your finished results will shine. Be slapdash, and your efforts will look ill-conceived and, ultimately, disappointing.

DO IT YOURSELF, BUT DO IT PROPERLY

Do what you can, but don't be a "have-a-go hero" if you're simply not up to the job at hand. Think about how much you'd save if you could actually rewire, tile or swap out a roof, then estimate how much wasted time and cash there'd be if your home became a series of botched jobs. In a nutshell, if DIY is not your thing, then try DFY: Done for You. Time to call in the pros…

KEEP VALUABLE SPACE FOR LIVING, NOT STORAGE

If storage quarters exist, use them. Should matters begin to overflow, consider investing in a separate garden shed, or convert a corner in the basement to provide a useful stash zone for the paraphernalia we all seem to accumulate. This practice frees up valuable life-space, whilst tempting focused design in rooms that are used most frequently. Cleaning and clearly defining space costs nothing, so lose the clutter and try to keep rooms "single-function." However, if you have to house a home office, for example (perhaps in a bedroom), endeavour to keep the trappings of work in a closed armoire or cupboard, out of sight when not in use.

MOVE THINGS AROUND

Sometimes a change of orientation is all that's needed to freshen proceedings and proffer a whole new look. This in mind, move your sofa to the other side of the room, try the bed on another wall or simply clear clutter and rearrange accessories to re-dress your space.

USE WHAT YOU'VE GOT

Raid the attic; fish out an old family dresser and give it a facelift. A lick of paint and some new handles could make it worthy of being centre stage once again. Similarly, add shelves to a dated armoire and transform it into a media centre. Or reach for the sewing machine and make slipcovers for an old sofa. Always think out of the box and, wherever possible, learn to look at things differently.

SWAP SKILLS

Ok, so you're handy with a sewing machine but know nothing about electrics. So what are you going to do about your terrible cabin lighting? Hold on: your next-door neighbour's a friendly electrician, but he has terrible curtains. Offer to make him some new drapery in exchange for fitting some overhead lighting? Think about swapping skills with friends, family and neighbours as a way of "paying" for home improvements.

SEARCH OUT "SCRATCH AND DENT"

Ask around larger furniture stores to discover whether they offer discounts on lightly damaged items, customer returns or even last season's stock. Some department stores have dedicated clearance centres, so it's worth scouting around. Remember this: it's not how much money you spend, but how you spend it that makes the biggest difference.

INVEST IN A HERO PIECE

It's worth shelling out a little bit extra for comfort—you want the best sofa and bed that you can afford—and on key pieces like branded kitchen appliances that set the scene for overall quality.

USE THE INTERNET

Swap, sell or search, and scour the Internet for bargains. Not only is there a world of opportunity at your fingertips, but you'll also save money by avoiding the gas costs associated with driving around trying to find those deals. Bear in mind, however, there may be delivery costs when you total up your spend . . .

SEASONAL ADJUSTMENT

Wherever possible, design space with a neutral backbone and choose relatively plain wall coverings and furniture. Then switch up your overall look with cleverly selected accessories. Remember, it's cheaper to change "decorative jewellery" than reconfigure a whole room so, if you're a habitual re-designer, let the seasons guide you: tailor your vibe with textiles to keep your cabin fresh for less.

The Escapes

The connection to the Scottish Highlands, provided by the placement of the
building and the use of glass to allow
occupants to experience their surroundings, gives this small space a huge
amount of heart and soul.

AirShip 002

LOCATION
Drimnin, Highlands,
Scotland

COMPLETION YEAR
2018

OWNERS
Roderick James and
Amanda Markham

ARCHITECT
Roderick James
Architects

CONTRACTOR
Out of the Blue

SIZE
388 sf (36 sqm)

NOTABLE BUILDING MATERIALS
Aluminum with foamcore-insulated
panels, double glazing, internal wood
cladding

UTILITIES
Electricity (standard supply and
back-up photovoltaic/solar power),
water (spring water and rainwater
piped from the roof to a reservoir
underneath the floor), waste (septic
system and compost toilet).

PHOTOGRAPHY
Nigel Rigden

Seriously, just *look* at this place. Perched as it is, high on a remote
outcropping overlooking the Isle of Mull and the Atlantic
Ocean, it's a wildly fascinating affair that intrigues and captivates from first inspection. Stoically attached to barren Scottish
landscape where sheep graze, deer wander and eagles soar is a
commanding aluminum capsule: a dramatic geometry of crystal-
clear, faceted glass that simply *aches* to be explored. Indeed,
AirShip 002 has landed. But what *is* it?

Appearing to have tumbled from the pages of a Philip Pull-
man novel, AirShip 002 is a shelter like no other. It's a very
remote, five-hour drive from Glasgow on single-track roads that
snake around stunning lochs and incredible scenery, but the
destination is worth the journey. Part late-nineteenth-century
Zeppelin, part 1930s airstream and part 1950s B-movie retro
spaceship, the structure might seem to be of alien origin—but

1. The aeronautical styling looks especially strong at dusk, when the interior glows from within and the pod genuinely looks like it's about to take off.

2. Get up and glow—the multi-windowpane construction gives the pod the appearance of a multi-faceted lamp by night—a warming beacon to welcome you in from the cold.

suffice to say, it definitely comes in peace. Or perhaps that should be *pieces* . . . thanks to its prefabricated self-assembly components.

Thoughtfully designed so that each of its building components can be carried by two people (to ease construction issues in even the trickiest spot), the remarkable building serves as one of the latest instalments in architect Roderick James's mission to create quality, ultra-livable small spaces that boast impressively energy-efficient credentials.

"When designing the AirShip," explains James, "my ambition was to create an unusual, even *iconic*, structure, with a thoroughly exciting glazing system. But it was also planned, from the outset, to be low maintenance. A key intention was that it could be erected in a week or so, and taken apart, were that ever required, in a similar time frame."

As one who likes to practice what he preaches, James built the AirShip on the property he shares with partner Amanda Markham. The couple use it as guest accommodation for friends

1. We've landed! AirShip 002 is positioned to enjoy the westerly views to the Ardnamurchan Peninsula and the Atlantic Ocean and easterly views towards the Isle of Mull. The aluminum pod is a lightweight and transportable prospect for anyone looking to create a remote getaway.

2. Working from home has never been this attractive. This room with a view is positive, encouraging and rewarding—everything you'd want from a home-office space.

3. The cool appearance of the aluminum and the warmth of the timber strike a delightful balance, creating a modern, welcoming space.

4. The pod is a lesson in making every inch of space count. Here, the overhead shower drains below the floor to keep the wet room from puddling.

5. The curtaining partitions off the bed, providing privacy and shelter from daylight to feel like a first-class bunk in an exotic train or airplane. The void underneath the bed provides valuable storage space.

and family (can you imagine popping by for a weekend and being tucked in here?) and as a "tiny house" Airbnb. With an interior fit out that offers a carefully specified inventory of furniture, it's basic, sure, but it's more than comfortable.

Everything is beautifully sandwiched between multi-paned "dragonfly" windows at either end, which flood the space with light whilst affording stunning views to the rolling Scottish countryside within which the unusual building nestles.

As Scots, we can attest that winters in our homeland's rural parts can be harsh, but AirShip's glass-and-aluminum frame is designed to withstand the elements with its aerodynamic form, set upon two oak supports that can easily resist the locale's oft' force 11 winds without movement. This, therefore, is one Air-Ship that will *never* take to the skies.

Whilst James maintains his project was designed for "pure, simple fun," it delivers *so* much more than his original ambition. It's a fantasy prism, whose unexpected architectural discipline, coupled with its location, creates a dynamic experience that's all about looking at things differently whilst immersed in the unusual. Sure, the surrounding topography is special, but as viewed through multi-paned windows, it appears decidedly more focused, even magical.

Inside, the spell continues. Space is imaginatively arranged to accommodate sleeping quarters, where privacy can be afforded by curtains (or light baffling, to soothe eyes following

one too many whiskies), a sitting area, a kitchen, a washroom and an office nook.

As an Airbnb property, over three hundred guests have delivered glowing online reviews with typical comments reporting it as "romantic," "exciting," "cosseting" and "stimulating." Simple words, perhaps, but prose, nonetheless, that captures the essence of the destination. To assemble such an exciting architectural vision is one thing, but to watch as it somehow merges with a ravaged landscape is another thing altogether.

As champions of structure that is individual, we've always encouraged buildings that are in any way left of field. AirShip is so popular, in fact, that the couple have been selling the kits so that anyone can have their own pod and are currently building a two-storey, aluminum-clad elliptical Pilot House, which will also be available to rent in the future.

As far as we can see, in the world of AirShip 002, any land can become a landing strip and you can pop one wherever you want to touch down. As a lesson in thinking out of the box, AirShip 002 demonstrates that the sky really is the limit!

1. The multi-faceted view through the multi-paned "dragonfly" windows accentuates the undulation of the rolling hills beyond.

2. The kitchen, outfitted to look like a cross between a retro American diner and a ship's galley, is loaded with smart small-space ideas: the wall-pocket storage, the folding kitchen table off the kitchen peninsula and the stools that act as dining chairs and occasional tables throughout.

3. A succession of portholes on the sides of the pod add to the project's individual style and allude to the appearance of a submarine. Besides, who doesn't want to be submersed in nature?

4. Every home should have a book nook—a comfortable corner to tuck yourself away and enjoy a good read. This one is ideal.

It's hard not to be drawn to the structure's external skin: the "envelope" is a combination of prefabricated, insulated walls and roofing panels with strong visual contrast delivered by the dual-toned finish. We particularly like the combo of pale wood and dramatic black: it's visually commanding and amply references the currently popular vernacular of a modern-rustic style.

The Backcountry Hut

LOCATION
Vancouver, British
Columbia, Canada

CONCEPT YEAR
2017

ARCHITECT
The Backcountry Hut
Company

SIZE
700 sf (65 sqm)

NOTABLE BUILDING MATERIALS
Engineered timber frame,
prefabricated insulated wall, roof,
and floor panels

UTILITIES
A choice of on-grid supply that can
be customized to meet "Net Zero
Energy" standards

PHOTOGRAPHY
Courtesy of The Backcountry
Hut Company

Oh, how the (previously) humble prefabricated cabin has changed. Aye, the notion of self-assembled kit houses isn't necessarily groundbreaking, but the way in which The Backcountry Hut Company has reimagined the concept certainly is.

Launched in 2015, the firm was birthed to satisfy what its founders saw as a gap in the market for simple recreational structures. Structures that could be easily installed in even the most remote, abandoned locations.

It's an idyll about which we (and many backcountry enthusiasts) have long since romanticized. However, having presided over (and negotiated the construction programs of) many isolated projects, we know only too well how difficult it can be to strategize timings, crews, tradespeople and the requisite materials to fashion our oft' ambitious wilderness dreams. And while many other developers with less sturdy constitutions might have jumped from the transformative train when attempting to establish their rural credentials, we were hell-bent on making it all work. (Hmm—if only The Backcountry Hut Company had

existed when we were starting out, our initial projects might have been somewhat easier to strategize.)

Appraising market shortcomings and the commercial opportunities therein, Backcountry Hut Company founder Wilson Edgar—together with architect Michael Leckie and Swiss master builder Cyrill Werlen—conspired a modular system that allowed the containing walls, floors and roofs of their cabins to be proportionally tailored to meet the spatial requirements of individual clients.

1. The frame is composed of sustainably harvested, engineered timber with an architectural "cut out" that forms a covered porch area to the rear and a sheltered deck area at the front.

Uncomplicated "nail-in" windows are provided as part of the kit and these are further secured when the prefabricated cladding is applied. Windows, like many aspects of the hut, can be sized and tailored to suit location, to take advantage of views or to amplify illumination in a darker area.

Crucially, much of the work can be done, by the manufacturer, off-site, so that on-site self-assembly is eminently simpler than a standard build. Think flat pack on a giant scale. Ikea to the power of ten? Yes, but worry not about locating behemoth-sized Allen keys and specifically skilled partners: the structures can be erected by those with regular construction skills using everyday tools.

Fully customizable, and manufactured with a zero-waste philosophy, the basic shell consists of four posts, four beams and a roof, with environmentally sustainable products used at every stage of manufacture. The company maintains that their product is ideal for "barn raisings"—group builds which draw requisite labour from the local community. It's an old-school notion that really appeals to us.

When communities rally, a sense of pride develops, which, from our experience, fosters a sense of overall project commitment. We've long subscribed to the worth of shopping local; building local, as we see it, follows the same notion of drawing from one's nearby skill set to pull together that homely dream—only on a much bigger scale.

The appeal of these buildings is definitely on the rise. Perhaps this increased demand can be attributed to the fact that, as a world, we've become ever more "off the shelf" insofar as expectation and availabilities are concerned. Many of us want things quickly, in the shortest order time possible, with easy deliveries and no, or few, questions asked.

But with this burgeoning demand for an easy ride will come eventual tedium and a boredom with the everyday or "expected." That's why we see custom upholstery, pre-measured suiting and personal tailoring on the rise. And why the notion of "bespoke" has garnered growing appeal across many industries—from international travel to car detailing, from restaurants to entertainment. It's a cause-and-effect response to the humdrum. Put simply, it's a retaliation against the everyday, and the reason why The Backcountry Hut Company is growing so quickly...

1. The building has a steep pitched roof, an aesthetic that exudes strong, contemporary relevance. But the shell shape is about so much more than visuals: its dynamic pitch helps deflect the elements, particularly the gathering of snow in colder environments.

2. The structure is designed to sit on piles, rather than a foundation, so its positioning, generally speaking, will have less impact on the environment. In essence, it's normally easier and less costly to install piers than it is full foundations or a poured concrete basement.

If terrain is rocky, limited drilling may be required to secure piers, but if ground is softer, concrete sonotubes may be sufficient. For these, the ground will need to be lightly excavated, then cardboard tubes will be inserted and concrete poured in to facilitate a solid grip.

Texture is the new colour—corrugated
steel cladding and a raised-seam
metal roof accent the straight line of
this exciting cabin.

Blackbirch

LOCATION
Haliburton, Ontario,
Canada

COMPLETION YEAR
2012

OWNERS
Chris and Susan Meiorin
and Mia the Vizsla

ARCHITECT
STAMP Architecture

INTERIOR DESIGNERS
Chris and Susan Meiorin
in association with
Brad Netkin of STAMP
Architecture

CONTRACTOR
Level Design Build

SIZE
2,400 sf (223 sqm)

NOTABLE BUILDING MATERIALS
Douglas fir beams, corrugated steel
and Maibec pre-finished wood siding,
wood plank flooring, maple panel
ceilings, extensive barnboard interior
detailing, euro + glasshaus windows
and doors

UTILITIES
Electricity (on-grid supply), gas
(propane), heating (radiant in-floor
heating), water (well), waste (septic
system)

PHOTOGRAPHY
Courtesy of STAMP Architecture

It's fair to suggest that, by now, most of us know about making a style statement courtesy of the little black dress. But how about delivering similarly stylish impact with a big, black, dramatically attired cabin? Blackbirch, perched as it is on a tree-covered granite outcropping in Haliburton, manages to do precisely that.

A commanding affair with sombre steel cladding, stark rectilinear lines and expansive use of glass, it's an undoubted architectural fantasy, yet one—for all its modernity—that's welcoming at every turn, with an exterior that in no way overwhelms its environment.

Owners Chris and Susan Meiorin designed their 2,400-sf (223-sqm) bolthole in association with Brad Netkin of Toronto's STAMP Architecture, their combined efforts delivering the

perfect backdrop for weekend retreats, summer vacations and family gatherings.

"In the city," enthuses Chris, whilst making coffee for our assembled team, "we seem to be eternally busy, always running, so we just eat when we can. But at the lake, it's all about sharing. Food, for us, is a *huge* pleasure and we love to experiment." Susan picks up: "And when not gathered around a table, we're out on the boat, weather permitting, or swimming in the lake. Coming here nurtures decompression in us all. It truly is our happy place."

Arranged over two principal levels (with a laundry and TV room in the basement), Blackbirch is stoically clad in corrugated-steel panelling set under a raised-seam metal roof. On the main floor, a spacious kitchen, a comfortable living area, a well-appointed dining zone and a semi-outdoor screened room mesh as an incredible sharing space.

In the Blackbirch kitchen, steel appliances and handles punctuate the inky darkness of the streamlined cabinetry. The

1. The creation of two separate areas—one for living and one for sleeping—gives guests a choice. If the party goes a little too late, revellers can retreat through the door in the barnboard wall to chill in the comfortably arranged sleeping quarters that lie behind. Each guest nook is simply appointed, but amply caters to overnight requirements. There's a sublimely unfussy vibe in these quarters, but it's from this casual dressing that the rooms draw their strength.

2. The staircase is almost invisible thanks to open-tread steps and a frameless glass banister.

1. Incorporating a screened-in porch, if possible—large enough to serve as a dining room and ancillary lounge area—is super important, particularly during Canada's warmer months. That feeling of being outside yet immune to entomological attack is veritably joyous.

What's more, a screened porch allows the calendar to stretch, insofar as being outdoors when Mother Nature's summery charms yield to cooler autumn breaths. Add a space heater and a few cozy throws, and alfresco dining (and reclining) can continue well beyond normal calendar expectation.

room, Chris and Susan being devoted foodies, is packed with every conceivable convenience to enhance the gastronomic adventure: from blenders, whizzers and choppers to dicers, slow cookers and sous-vide apparatus, it's all there, neatly stored in generous cupboards.

"We do a lot of food prep in here," explains Susan, "but we also have a wood-burning oven in the garden that turns out pizza, fish and seafood, sausage, meats and veggies *all* year round." Matters Bacchanalian aside, there's no doubt about it, it's a party house as much as it's a home. And that's just how its owners like it. The entire Meiorin family, in fact, works hard to ensure guests are indulged at *every* turn.

"We hold wine tastings throughout the year with friends who have cabins on the lake or guests who're staying here with us. They're always super interesting and educational, especially when paired with food—it's the ideal sharing experience."

1. Massive spans of euro + glasshaus windows and doors encase the entire cabin, and the windows tilt (or open fully) to allow ventilation in the absence of mechanical air conditioning.

2. The centrally positioned wood-burning stove creates an attractive and functional focal point that warms the dining and kitchen areas *and* the living zone that sits to the other side. In the cottage context, few things are more atmospheric than the intoxicating aroma of a crackling log fire. Whether yours is a towering stone-built chimney, a modest traditional hearth or a contemporary incarnation such as this one, "flame on," say we.

1. Beyond the barnboard living-room wall lies a comfortable inner sanctum with bedrooms and washrooms. The lower ceiling and pale shiplap-clad walls punctuate the rustic vibe that permeates the principal areas in Blackbirch.

2. In vacation respites like Blackbirch, bedrooms don't have to be overly large, or comparable to those you'd expect to find in a principal home. Precisely how much, after all, do your guests plan on bringing? When designing cottages, we tend to max up on the comfort quotient rather than overplay closets and wardrobes. Invitees, generally speaking, are more likely to enjoy a great bed and a cozy chair than a room compromised by oversized closets.

On the opposite side of the room, across a landscape of contemporary furniture—and past a striking drum-shaped vertical log stove—is a two-storey high wall of grey barnboard whose beautiful texture infuses the overall aesthetic with a nod to the past, whilst contrasting with the smooth blond timber panels that clad the ceiling. The barnboard wall, beautiful in its own right, delineates the primary shared living zone from the sleeping quarters (and washrooms), which are arranged across the ground and top floors.

Statement glazing features prominently (Chris owns euro + glasshaus, one of North America's busiest and certainly most highly regarded fenestration companies) with tilt-action framework planted within every elevation to welcome in—or indeed baffle—lake breezes and keep the climate wonderfully cool.

Ah, yes, "cool": climatically, stylistically and everything in between. From the large-scale Scrabble set that adorns the dining table to a statement turntable that crowns the entertainment station, designer aplomb permeates everything. Self-confirmed vinyl junkies, we take a moment to scan the album stock and find it unsurprisingly eclectic. From old favourites like Grace Jones, Blondie and Elton John to albums by the Tragically Hip, Massive Attack and Madonna, it's all there for guests to plunder and enjoy.

As we see it, Chris and Susan embody a new type of luxury: one that's less about gold taps and marble pillars and more about the subtle art of restraint, quality materials, environmental harmony and atmosphere. As Chris says: "For me, it's the chance to be with my family. And with my friends. Blackbirch provides the perfect platform for us all to decompress." Susan picks up the point: "For all of us, it's about the quiet, the fresh air and that clear, clean lake. We love our city life, but this is different. This place takes us to the next level."

The simple cabin with a big heart—
the modest exterior blends
perfectly into the landscape, as
seamlessly as the trees.

Bridger Canyon Guest House

LOCATION
Bozeman, Montana, USA

COMPLETION YEAR
2017

OWNERS
Brad and Stacey
Beckworth

ARCHITECT
Miller-Roodell
Architects

INTERIOR DESIGNER
Abby Hetherington
Interiors

CONTRACTOR
Bolton Custom Homes

SIZE
1,665 sf (155 sqm)

NOTABLE BUILDING MATERIALS
Wood post-and-beam frame,
timber siding, reclaimed internal
wood walls and stone chimney,
all set under a raised-seam metal
roof

UTILITIES
On-grid supply

PHOTOGRAPHY
Audrey Hall

The notion of a "curated" home is hugely appealing. You know, a place where everything is expertly specified to contribute to the final vision: a thoughtful production where no detail is left unconsidered, no schematic opportunity missed.

But, of course, layering is everything. In the curated sphere, it's all about establishing a perfect fusion of architecture, materials and finishes so that beauty, functionality and personality can effortlessly merge. The Bridger Canyon Guest House in Bozeman, Montana, is one such home.

When Texans Brad and Stacey Beckworth finally settled on the ideal spot for their ultimate retreat (after an extensive

fourteen-year search), they knew its realization would be hugely rewarding. Boasting 270 acres of diverse land (straddling rocky outcrops, hayfields and wetlands), the estate can best be described as magical. Little wonder, then, they fell in love with the awe-inspiring valley land and its sense of calm isolation from their very first inspection.

Ambitious to the max, they made a bid and held their breath. With the site secured, the adventurous couple hired Miller-Roodell Architects to play out their vision: a modern retreat with vast expanses of glazing, a spacious barn and an ancillary cottage to provide comfortable accommodation for overnight guests.

To get their family on site quickly, the Beckworths put their primary efforts into the modest guest cabin, a new building constructed with locally curated elements to add a handcrafted, historically-relevant feel. Imagine re-creating a vintage car, from scratch, using new parts—that's the story of the guest annex, a new build suffused with a prevailing sense of nostalgia and authenticity.

First inspection reveals a modest structure with a carport set behind. Lines are low, symmetrical and assembled on a cross-axis, with the project sheltered at the rear by a wooded slope but open at the front to embrace the expansive views. But whilst everything has been composed to seem as unfussy as possible, an overwhelming sense of care and considered planning prevails.

A simple palette of wood siding, dark metal roofing and cool stone bows to the cabin's natural surroundings, rather than attempting to dominate the landscape, an important consideration in a new build project such as this. The operative word being "blend."

Another crucial factor is engaging sympathetic team players to assemble the vision. Fifth-generation carpenter Cass Bolton hand-picked the multicoloured wood panelling that warms the exterior and the uniformly grey indoor panelling that serves as a serene backdrop for the oh-so-cool interior design.

Modestly scaled at just 1,665 sf (155 sqm), that interior is nonetheless inspiring. The backdrop of weathered timber, metal countertops, a fireplace made of Montana moss rock (a term used to describe fieldstone collected in central Montana) and

1. The recipe for this kitchen space, featuring wood walls, ceilings and cabinets, metal countertops and concrete flooring, is cabin perfection. Smart and practical, you can almost smell the apple pies being baked here.

2. A wonderfully simple welcome—just leave your boots and jacket at the door and come right in.

concrete floors provided the perfect backdrop for designer Abby Hetherington to curate a space that's rich in fabrics, art, exquisite furniture, timber and tile. Simplicity, as we see it, is this cabin's watchword: courtesy of an unstinting roster of quality layers, expertly installed to elicit a quiet, informal feel, Hetherington has infused the project with endless atmosphere.

The perfect storm of architect, contractor and designer—plus clients with a talent for collecting special things—serve a thoroughly individual experience, one which positively oozes chic. Vintage photographs and Montana history books weave a sense of past, whilst Yellowstone National Park memorabilia, antique lamps, textural rugs and repurposed objects telegraph a sense of legacy. It's quite an achievement in a new-build cabin.

In the kitchen, reclaimed timber merges doors into walls, whilst a custom range hood and backsplash tile bolster a warmly aesthetic mood. Comfort and conviviality are certainly key: log stacks, roaring fires and inviting sofas gather to offer guests a warm, and eminently friendly, hug.

1. In this living room, casual elegance abounds thanks to an inviting sofa by Verellen, a Ralph Lauren table lamp and a Robert Ogden floor lamp. Extending the space outdoors is a timbered, gabled structure which partially shades a covered patio.

2. A warm welcome awaits—when the mercury plummets, the Montana moss rock fireplace serves as a cozy gathering point for guests.

The Bridger Canyon Guest House is a perfect jewel, a precious cabin that's sure to appeal to visitors. Courtesy of beautiful wood cladding and generous antique detailing, it's gorgeous to look at, but it's about so much more than that: it's about atmosphere and the awareness that it was created by joyfully skilled hands, hands that toiled over every detail to curate a layered world with heart, soul and history.

1. The homeowners wanted their cabin to feel eclectic, and the *Buffalo Nickel* artwork by Andy Warhol more than speaks to this ambition. Modern art shouldn't be the exclusive preserve of modern homes—mixing traditional and contemporary styles is a surefire way to create an individual look.

2–3. Galvanized wall sconces add a tough, barn-like feel, whilst chunky cabinet hardware adds weight to the reclaimed timber doors.

The graphic floor tiles suffuse a little Aztec feel in the bathroom while the sliding reclaimed-wood door adds extra texture.

4. A custom wood cabinet is topped with a concrete trough sink and dressed with antler light pendants. Meanwhile, the bright modern chair provides a pop of colour.

The restrained exterior provides
little clue as to the layered and decidedly indulgent joys that lie within.

The Bunker

LOCATION
Yellowstone Club,
Montana, USA

COMPLETION YEAR
2017

OWNERS
Hap and Sue Brakeley

ARCHITECT
Miller-Roodell Architects

INTERIOR DESIGNER
Abby Hetherington
Interiors

CONTRACTOR
On Site Management

SIZE
10,348 sf (961 sqm)

NOTABLE BUILDING MATERIALS
Native rock and reclaimed wood
connected with oversized glass

UTILITIES
Electricity (geothermal), gas
(propane), water (on-grid supply),
waste (septic system)

PHOTOGRAPHY
David O. Marlow

Well, there's no doubt about it: the Bunker is a *large* proposition. A *very* large proposition indeed at more than 10,000 sf (929 sqm). Yet for all the respite's enormity, it manages, against all the odds, to feel intimate and cosseting at every turn—and thoroughly at home (for all its modernistic leanings and Jurassic scale) on its terrain.

Envisioned as a unique home from home in which owners Sue and Hap Brakeley and their six adult children could live their best lives during holidays, family celebrations and downtime, it's a *staggeringly* beautiful affair. And so it should be: its realization is the result of long-term planning and auspicious organization.

With the intention of spending half the year there (the remaining portion of the calendar in Florida), Sue and Hap

dreamed of a home that would cater to their hobbies, which include skiing, golfing and entertaining.

The beautiful mountain retreat is constructed from locally sourced rock and acres of textural reclaimed lumber. Arranged to the side of a fairway at Montana's Yellowstone Club (where the couple previously owned a condo) and featuring large-scale glazing, specified to embrace the breathtaking views of Montana's famous "Big Sky," the structure is a symphony of rectilinear form that captivates from every elevation.

The visionary hired by the Brakeleys was Joe Roodell, of Bozeman-based Miller-Roodell Architects, whose remit was to devise a footprint that would embrace the versatile landscape upon which the ranch-like structure would eventually sit.

"It was this bridge of two different environments," Joe explains, "from the manicured golf course to the ruggedness of the

1. The deliberate sense of asymmetry is the first thing to catch the eye in this well-appointed room. Since time immemorial, designers have crafted mirror-image vignettes, knowing that many clients find "balance" reassuring. That said, there's something satisfying about forgoing balance, the ethos working particularly well where "eclectic" reigns and where multiple messages conspire to create the overall vision. The portrait of a family member painted by renowned nineteenth-century artist Thomas Sully was a great starting point, with further off-balance signalling arriving via other artworks and the positioning of furniture.

2. Was there ever a kitchen more deserving of the title "rugged"? This space, as we see it, is a show-stopper. We love the woodsy mix: from the oak flooring to the chunky overhead lumber, and from the island's hefty wood construction to the rough beams surrounding the connecting room aperture, it's all beautiful. The metal-faced cabinetry simply amplifies the rugged appeal, but it's balanced by the softer wood facing that clads the connecting corridor. This room is a triumph, huh?

3. Now you see it, now you don't. Situated in the main living space, the ingenious home bar is where the Brakeleys do most of their entertaining. When guests depart, however, one-click retractable steel covers conceal the gantry shelving.

The bar, as we see it, is a work of art. Created by MFGR Designs, a horizontal metal slab, cantilevered from the wall, provides ample surface around which barflies can gather. Support, at the opposite end, comes via a large chunk of spalted wood (wood discoloured by fungi), the organic nature of which serves as a vertical foil to the horizontal elevation.

mountains, that appealed." Appraising the project for a moment, he continues, "We wanted to bring those aspects together, so we straddled the ridge and accomplished that through form."

And what a form it is. Colossal in volume, the cabin includes a collection of four principal suites, a junior suite, a bunk-bed room for the grandchildren, a theatre room, and generous living, dining and kitchen areas. And then there's that dreamy outdoor deck, terrace and patio space, masterfully composed to embrace the commanding views that sprawl in every direction.

Designing and building from scratch, rather than retooling an existing home, allowed Sue and Hap to configure the space to suit their lives, rather than contend with the hereditary framework of previous owners. First up, as admirers of the open-concept model, they elected to position a free-flowing living, dining and entertaining area on the main floor, with bedrooms discreetly positioned to afford guests (and hosts) measured privacy.

As designers who've embellished literally *hundreds* of client homes, the two of us tend (for the most part, certainly) to sing

1. Eclectic is certainly order of the day in the principal living area. A commanding bison bust and a chandelier fashioned from deer antlers set a heady tone. Meanwhile, *Cowboy* (by Wallace Piatt), a strikingly colourful piece, lends the environment a tongue-in-cheek Western vibe.

2. A compendium of modern artwork enlivens this woodsy environment with splashes of colour.

from the same hymn book when it comes to vision. Hap and Sue, however, have differing styles that, for other partnerships, could have served as a stumbling block to moving ahead. Hap admires traditional wooden beams and barnboard, whilst Sue is predisposed to more modernist leanings.

But of course discussion, played patiently, can coax compromise, and the delivery of a shared vision. Suitably informed, the couple's design team merged indigenous local rock and reclaimed wood, sanctioned with steel detailing and contemporary lines to satisfy *each* of their clients' predilections. And somehow it all merges seamlessly to deliver an aesthetic that's at once "of the land" and contemporary.

With their interior configurations complete, Hap and Sue engaged designer Abby Hetherington to add a sense of fun and levity. At her clients' behest, Hetherington fused a vibrant and eclectic mix of art, indulgent fabrics and clever lighting to play in friendly contrast to the structural palette of the home's Western materials.

1. A confident mix of fur, fringe and pattern amplifies the touchy-feely quotient in the library, a room which feels for all the world like it was plucked from a Spanish villa in Los Feliz, Los Angeles. Floating above, like some steampunked, crash-landed sputnik, is a Kirsten Kainz chandelier, imaginatively assembled from a cute collection of *objets trouvés* and discarded toys.

2. It's hard not to enjoy the whimsy of the upcycled globe light fixture (made by True North Forge) that hangs in this guest suite.

Via textiles and furnishings, shots of Hermès orange are interspersed with pink and a palette of blue. It's an impressive schematic landscape, for sure, as one "compartment" yields to the next with each zone every bit as welcoming as that which went before. Layering is crucial: ceilings are embellished with pendulous light fittings, brightly hued carpets and rugs dispense floor-level colouration, and windows are dressed with immaculate pinch-pleated drapery on almost every elevation.

Since their project completed in 2017, the Brakeleys have hosted countless large dinners, several bustling parties and all manner of familial celebrations. Yet when the party finishes,

1–2. In a confident allusion to classic log cabins, wall elevations in the bunkroom and powder room are embellished with rustic wood detailing. This architectural reference and sense of whimsy ensure the overall mood remains relaxed and friendly. Stoic steel elements are served up via access ladders and side bars, their chunky nature delivering a sense of real permanence.

3. Wood-framed bunk beds, which provide extra sleeping space for grandchildren and overspill guests, have been lavished, to dramatic effect, with teal-blue paint.

4. MFGR Designs created the bespoke steel layering (the locker-room doors being one such aspect) that punctuate many areas in the beautiful getaway.

the space still feels cozy and atmospheric, and amply intimate for two.

Home construction, as we oft' opine—and decorating, thereafter—is a veritable science. But, like any science project, delicate balance can be so easily thrown if the ingredient list is in any way "off." The Bunker, however, for all its scale, and all its mixed messaging, is a veritable triumph. And the perfect observation of what can happen when clients, architects and interior designers work in harmony. It's the perfect stylistic trifecta. And when the magic *really* happens...

1. The master bedroom is an undoubted sanctuary for its inhabitants. Two generously proportioned Sao chairs by Los Angeles design team Jean de Merry fight a battle for the Kelly Wearstler table that sits between them, in front of a rectilinear stove and that jaw-dropping view.

2. The double vanity makes everyday bathing an event, whilst the mirrored wall tricks the eye into perceiving even more generous proportions than actually exist. The frames set "upon" the mirror amplify the wow factor and further the great act of visual deception.

3. This stand-alone vanity sets the tone, illustrating the power of a focal-point furniture piece. The industrial framework and stone sink are beautiful and functional: a truly twenty-first century addition.

A beacon of light in the darkness—the respite's glow offers a warm, homely welcome. The only electricity, however, comes via two solar panels that form part of the chimney cladding.

Cabin at Norderhov

LOCATION
Krokskogen Forest,
Norway

COMPLETION YEAR
2014

OWNERS
Clients of Atelier Oslo

ARCHITECT
Atelier Oslo

CONSULTANTS
Estatikk AS

CONTRACTOR
Byggmester Bård
Bredesen.

SIZE
538 sf (50 sqm)

NOTABLE BUILDING MATERIALS
Prefabricated wood structure
supported by steel rods drilled into
the rock and supplemented with
concrete foundations for stabilization;
exterior walls and roof clad in
overlapping stone plates

UTILITIES
Electricity (solar panels on the
chimney power LED lamps inside),
heating (wood-fired), water (from a
nearby river), waste (compost toilet)

PHOTOGRAPHY
Lars Petter Pettersen and Atelier Oslo

The most successful retreats—as we see it, certainly—are those which offer memorable experiences courtesy of location, architecture, finishes and, last but not least, the element of surprise. At Cabin at Norderhov, a seasonal retreat in Norway, the facade's rectangular geometry acts like a gift box proffering no clue to the surprising interior (which boasts more curves than a Formula One racetrack) concealed within.

As with so many getaways, location is everything, and the Norderhov project certainly doesn't disappoint: its windblown, steep-sloped position provides a commanding view over Lake Steinsfjorden and the verdant Krokskogen forest which lies beyond.

1. A place to reflect—the forest, mirrored in the fenestration, creates a camouflage effect, at dusk, against the verdant backdrop.

2. The cabin, for the most part, is assembled from prefabricated elements, a process which makes construction, especially in a difficult-to-reach site, much easier.

From our experience, it's fair to suggest that fortune favours the brave homebuilding contingent who face up to—and conquer—the landscape (and its attendant issues) to position their ideal escape against difficult odds. Here, being that the site is often exposed to strong winds, each of the outdoor decks and patios is protected by the shapes and forms of the building, yet designed to take full advantage of the sun at different times of the day. All of this is testament to the architect's understanding of the terrain and, just as importantly, the challenges faced as a consequence of climatic vagaries.

But that understanding of the climate doesn't stop at the front door. The appreciation, in fact, continues indoors, thanks to large expanses of floor-to-ceiling windows in the principal zones which, as well as letting in great swathes of light, serve up panoramic views of majestic Lake Steinsfjorden.

All this, of course, is in stark contrast to the sleeping area, an intimate nook where subtler levels of natural light nudge in from the glass facade and via a small ventilation window in the

1. The hideaway grows darker as residents move to the bedroom, the light from the glass facade and a small ventilation window creating a cocooning effect.

2. Inside, expansive glazing delivers connection to the woodland atmosphere and floods the birch-clad rooms with natural light and unbounded views of Lake Steinsfjorden.

northern corner. The concept being that, moving towards the bedroom, the hideaway grows darker and eminently more conducive to sleep.

Throughout the 538-sf (50-sqm) space, alternating depths are used to clearly define "function," with living, eating, bathing and sleeping mapped out perfectly in each of the cabin's "arms." Although comprising four clear functions, the interior seems to roll as one continuous space, with curved walls and softly undulating birch-clad ceilings that gently transition users from zone to zone.

So how did the cabin's curves come to be? Relatively simply, actually: a milled plywood skin was fashioned across a prefabricated wooden frame to define the geometry of the interior. Virtually devoid of rectilinear constraints, the smooth blond aesthetic is at once escapist and comforting, conveying the kind of mood that might be expected in a smooth-walled Middle Eastern desert home or, perhaps, in a respite on some far-distant

planet. Hey, listen carefully, and you might just hear Luke Sky-walker calling for Uncle Owen.

The cabin's focal point is undoubtedly the fireplace, a sculptural spout which pours from the ceiling before levitating, mid-air, over a round, glazed fire bowl that's encircled by hexagonal marble tiles. Positioned at the centre of the cabin—and set down in the floor of the main level—it feels like an indoor campfire, one that's navigable from all sides.

Nils Ole Bae Brandtzaeg of Atelier Oslo, the architects responsible for the unique building, says of the project: "It's like one large piece of furniture," and he's not far wrong. His reasoning resonates as we appraise the unique dwelling. As floor heights "transition" between zones, the resultant step-ups

1. Each of the cabin's four compartments branches from a central fireplace that acts as a campfire—a warming heart that offers refuge from the harsh Norwegian winds.

2. Curves yield to multi-leveled wall and ceiling surfaces, effectively blurring the lines between each zoned function.

3. A house where walls become furniture—custom elements enhance the architecture, keeping the overall vision as unadulterated as possible.

serve double duty as natural perches for lounging, whilst stairs become seats and useful surfaces upon which life is played out. It really is the ultimate in minimalism.

Whilst minimalism might be the architectural remit, a maximalist attachment to nature offers balance. Establishing a strong connection to the landscape is, of course, one of the main reasons to own an escape, and that ideology is abundantly clear at Norderhov. Being able to enjoy the cabin was one thing, but framing those killer views (with minimal obstruction) was paramount to the dream that resulted in such perfectly blurred lines between indoors and out.

The large glass walls in the living and dining areas, for example, are positioned in such a way as to make their frames

1. A repeating palette of stone, glass and timber creates a space that offers many functions, yet which connects—visually and ergonomically—as one.

2. The fireplace is framed with hexagonal marble tiles which transition, beyond, into birch log tiles.

3. A bowl sink continues the curved trend that echoes throughout. The architects installed a composting vacuum toilet that filters wastewater in special drainage ducts.

virtually invisible as viewed from inside. And in the kitchen, custom cabinets (designed by Atelier Oslo) are fashioned in the same lumber as the walls upon which they are fixed, essentially allowing them to recede, so the views beyond can be appreciated without distraction.

Outside, the roof is covered in basalt-stone slabs, arranged in a pattern similar to that which is often used for traditional Norwegian wood cladding. It is a mash-up of acute and obtuse angularity, paired with rectilinear and perpendicular lines to form the walls. Viewing the windowless rear elevation, the building looks more like a monument than it does a dwelling, with the irregular lines making it hard to determine where walls end and rooflines begin.

In summation, can a starkly attired, modern homestead deliver the warmth more typically associated with a traditional cabin? Well, if that homestead embraces its surroundings to meld with nature, and if its smooth lines and timbers can somehow echo the forest within which it sits, then yes, it can. And that twenty-first-century exterior might very well contain a traditional cabin heartbeat within. Now wouldn't that be a pleasant surprise?

1. As viewed from the rear, the structure looks more like a modern monument than a cabin.

2. Exterior walls are attired in basalt-stone slabs, arranged to echo traditional Norwegian wood cladding.

3. Built into the sloping landscape, the structure merges effortlessly with its surroundings

The statuesque carport is the first structure to greet visitors, with the combination of red brick and concrete providing a taste of what's to come.

Casa en el Bosque

LOCATION Santiago, Nuevo León, Mexico	**SIZE** 1,776 sf (165 sqm)
	NOTABLE BUILDING MATERIALS Concrete, steel, glass, clay brick
COMPLETION YEAR 2018	**UTILITIES** On-grid supply
OWNERS Clients of WEYES Estudio	**PHOTOGRAPHY** The Raws
ARCHITECT WEYES Estudio	
STRUCTURE DESIGNER CM Ingeniería y Estructuras	
CONTRACTOR Sagal Grupo Constructor	

Can a modernistic edifice, one composed of bleak concrete and visually unforgiving steel, blend, somewhat casually, into a woodsy, jungle-like environment? Can strong architectural form exist without throwing aside the verdant allure of nature by which it's surrounded? Perhaps yes, if the structure is Casa en el Bosque—a single-family home that consists of four small pavilions linked by a winding exterior walkway that seems to float above the forest upon which it's perched.

Appraising concrete as a medium used in the home-construction industry, it's all too easy to think of Brutalism—the modernistic movement characterized by monolithic, blocky shapes, rigid geometric style and the large-scale use of poured concrete.

1. The vertical steel posts echo the trunks of the trees as they branch out, offering support to the pavilion structure. The exposure of each length elongates the sense of height, making the structure appear taller.

2. The open concrete-box structure and outsized glass frontage combine to deliver a cloak of invisibility over the pavilion. Being surrounded by trees and having trees reflect in the glass gives the structure stealth appeal.

This property, though, is far from brutal. If you'll allow us a little wordplay, we'll invent the term "quadruplism," as the retreat features not one but *four* concrete pavilions. Located in a large forest just outside Santiago, Nuevo León, the fascinating "house in the forest" is suffused with a plethora of ingenious design features, each envisioned to ensure that the man-made complex sits comfortably in its forested context.

One of the first challenges facing the compound's architectural team was where, precisely, to position the cabin. The tiny plot, measuring less than 7,500 sf (697 sqm), is beset with rich vegetation and seventeen large-scale trees, so the cabin was built with light machinery to ensure minimal landscape disturbance.

Foundations were carefully placed to respect tree-root structure patterns, and the height of the architecture was exactingly calculated to respect the treetop canopy within which the house sits. By all accounts it was a painstaking task—especially

1. Custom floor-to-ceiling millwork adds both decor and function, with height and timber balancing the open views onto the trees beyond. The upward slope of the concrete ceiling embraces the views and seems to draw light into the interior. The extension of the visible steel frame from inside to out further enhances the blurring of where the interior ends and the exterior begins.

2. Simple comforts—a hammock on the roof provides a swinging vantage point to while away the hours.

3. The natural rawness of the concrete creates an organic, imperfect finish that complements its surroundings perfectly. The idea of a separate bedroom pod is exciting, especially when it's a symphony of glass and concrete and feels like the cozy version of a Bond villain's jungle lair.

given the fact that the house occupies a hillside with a variable inclination of between 30 and 40 percent.

A thoughtful mix of clay bricks (characteristically northeastern Mexican), exposed concrete, glass and metal help create the illusion that the boxy pods are suspended in branches, much like a tree house. The structure utilizes a traditional system of columns and concrete slabs, with double brick walls that extend, in places, into the landscape to create guide routes and semi-private outdoor patios.

Environmental awareness being at the forefront of this build, the design focuses on reducing daily consumption. The sloping, forest position takes advantage of tree shade and cross-ventilation to manage interior climate, thereby saving on cooling and heating costs, the latter further moderated by double walls which maintain temperatures during winter months. Furthermore, strategically placed windows and skylights illuminate the complex during the day, further reducing the need to use electric power.

Throughout, interior finishes combine natural elements with man-made detailing, whilst custom wood furniture invites extra warmth across the design landscape. Crucially, exterior and

interior landscapes are further connected by polished concrete floors and brick walls, both "repeating" or "echoing" elements serving to blur boundaries.

By building separate structures, all of which combine to form "one" dwelling, the architects have created a journey on which the transition from room to room involves heading outside and, therefore, interacting with nature. This makes even the simplest motion an experience. And of course because light, temperatures and atmosphere change as the day revolves, so too does the experiential transition itself.

As far as retreats go, this Mexican casa was clearly well planned, its realization the perfect observation of what can happen when client and architect toil in harmony. Yes indeed, it's a relaxed world: nothing seems forced. And perhaps surprisingly, for all its hard edges, the indulgent holiday home feels soft and welcoming, across its various zones, at every turn. Who knew that concrete could be a forest dweller's best friend?

1. The indoor/outdoor experience continues in the shower room, where a light well and the shadow of the trees create a pattern on the exterior concrete wall.

2. The lighting picks out both structure and nature as pathways and uprights are gently illuminated.

3. Lighting the bedroom pavilion from the rear floods the bed area with light and acts like a beacon to draw visitors in. From the outside, this reads as an offer of comfort and welcome. This is a place to leave your watch behind, leave the curtains open and awake with the creatures in the forest. The days are as long as the sun is …

A compendium of shapes and angles: the gravity-defying entranceway at FAHOUSE creates a show-stopping first impression.

FAHOUSE

LOCATION
Cantons-de-l'Est,
Quebec, Canada

COMPLETION YEAR
2016

OWNERS
Clients of Jean Verville

ARCHITECTS
Jean Verville in
association with Ulys
Collectif

CONTRACTOR
Ulys Collectif

SIZE
1,900 sf (177 sqm)

NOTABLE BUILDING MATERIALS
Hybrid concrete, steel and wood

UTILITIES
Electricity (on-grid supply), water
(well), waste (septic system)

PHOTOGRAPHY
Maxime Brouillet via v2com

Are you sitting comfortably? Then we'll begin. "Once upon a time there was an enchanted forest..." How many children's stories begin with a sentence like that? Hundreds? Thousands?

That which some might consider a fanciful idea for a storybook cabin was, in fact, the starting point for FAHOUSE: a picture-perfect modern retreat, nestled deep in an enveloping hemlock forest in Quebec's Eastern Townships.

Completed in 2016, the project was designed and created by Jean Verville as a weekend retreat for a professional couple and their children, a family who didn't want to buy a house off the peg, but rather something that would offer a more tailored approach to satisfying their lifestyle.

Unlike other storybook cabins, this one avoids being overly decorated, instead favouring a twenty-first-century take on the forest setting. Tall, angular and smartly attired in black, this is the Darth Vader of cabins, albeit with a much warmer heart.

Encompassing 1,900 sf (177 sqm), the three-storey house consists of two conjoined A-frame structures with jagged tips and black corrugated-steel cladding for extra intrigue. Imagine cutting house shapes from black cardstock and positioning them as part of some ominous forest diorama. Imagine that scene, for a moment, to appreciate the impact of this home as one dark shadow ghosts the next with unstinting sculptural efficiency.

Simple, yet at the same time incredibly sophisticated, the structure offers a wealth of architectural surprises. The front volume, for example, is perched atop a glass box with a portion of the ground level cut away, the resultant dramatic cantilever offering shelter as a large, terraced compartment.

The rear volume, on the other hand, reads as a tall, slender box with a substantial gabled roof. As a series of peaked shapes, each delivers on its own merit; but when clustered together, the sum of its parts is sculptural and playfully experiential.

This residence is a veritable feast of geometry, its triangular motifs the very backbone of the overall design, with seismic form that hugs the verdant slope of land to which it's attached. Illuminated at night, the front elevation appears to float, creating the kind of magic that's normally the preserve of fairy stories. It's a beacon of light—aglow and warming even from a distance.

The approach sends visitors down a wide staircase towards the aforementioned covered terrace. Through large glass doors,

1. Visitors entering into the living room and kitchen are met by a huge expanse of glass windows and doors that open out onto the sheltered patio.

2. On one side of the cabin, the roof slopes down, almost to ground level, and is neatly punctuated by two small, square windows.

3. The living area's continuous concrete floor, plywood ceiling and linear lighting design create an infinity effect from inside to out, punctuated only by the large glazed doors.

a welcoming reception area and an open-plan living/dining/kitchen space lie beyond. It feels indulgent, spacious and inviting at every turn.

Clearly defined, the cabin hub promotes generous sightlines to the surrounding landscape thanks to sliding doors that wrap around the entire lower facade, inviting access to, and immersion in, the forest. Baltic plywood features throughout, the matching kitchen appearing to recede into the blond timber backdrop like some magical architectural vanishing act.

The same finish across the floors, walls and ceilings creates a mirrored effect, and whilst we're perhaps more accustomed to swimming pools being described as "infinity," the infinity transition in this cottage seamlessly blurs the boundaries between indoors and out.

Adjacent to and above the main living area is a dedicated space for the family, the ground level dedicated to the younger contingent with extra bunk beds for sleepovers and easy access to playtime in the "enchanted forest" that lies just beyond the

1–2. Throughout, Baltic plywood panels and cabinetry elicit a calming mood—but to arrest the tranquil "beat," and for schematic punctuation, the mudroom is painted in a popping shade of raspberry pink.

3. Bringing carefully curated heritage pieces into an otherwise minimalist space allows them to be enjoyed without interruption.

sliding doors. Things are a little more adult-oriented on the second floor, where parents can escape to a timber-clad ensuite bedroom, a sanctuary of natural calm. Further stress-busting is delivered thanks to wide floor-to-ceiling windows that overlook the dense 360 degrees of forest that wrap around the home. Then there's that large bath that takes forest bathing to—literally—new heights. Aye, it really is like living in a veritable tree canopy.

And then, just when visitors might least expect it, the mood changes. Dramatically. Travel to the attic floor and an entirely new beat is introduced via white-painted finishes. This simple colour choice creates an ethereal and expansive feel in what could be a rather busy room, architecturally speaking, due to all those exposed beams, supports and cross members. Painting them unifies and softens the proceedings, thereby providing a clean and flexible environment for the family to enjoy.

The success story of this escape, we suppose, is one of simplicity; an uncomplicated colour palette and pared-back finishes create a balanced and singular vision. Here, colour comes from the family, their friends and from the landscape that surrounds the cabin. It's a functional stage for all of the many and varied adventures life has to offer. And that's one storybook tale of which we'll never tire.

1, 3. Spaces are lightly furnished to keep the focus on the natural palette outdoors.

2. The impressive family shower room is perfect for children's bath-time bubble battles, being that it's wrapped, from floor to ceiling, in easy-care tiles.

The flood-defense walls were built using local stone-stacking techniques to blend with the original building. When dealing with heritage properties, it's important to use relevant construction materials to complement existing style and create a sense of belonging.

Filly Island

LOCATION
Filly Island, Cirencester,
United Kingdom

COMPLETION YEAR
2015

OWNER
Mouse Martin

ARCHITECT
Cotswold Architects

CONTRACTOR
Cotswold Architects

SIZE
400 sf (37 sqm) including porch

NOTABLE BUILDING MATERIALS
Local Cotswold stone and timber-
beam construction set under a
natural slate roof

UTILITIES
On-grid supply

PHOTOGRAPHY
Unique Homestays

Imagine warm summer evenings, sitting on that beautiful wall, feet dangling in the softly moving stream. Add in a jug of Pimm's, homemade canapés and an aural backdrop of the river, the breeze in the trees, ducks quacking and bees buzzing. Bliss.

The original structure, built around 1750 using local Cotswold stone, provided the basis for this unique barn conversion that fuses past with present, courtesy of the owner's eclectic approach to renovation and interior styling. In its first incarnation, a tiny barn was built upon its own island, with a flowing river to one side and a mill stream to the other. Its location, we learn, was originally chosen for practical (rather than beautiful) reasons, being that it was built to shelter a horse whose job it was to pull a cart along the river. (Hence the property's name, Filly Island.)

Livable history is something that really fascinates us: the idea that a 250-year-old building can be so successfully transformed into a contemporary retreat (without sacrificing its

1. If you have outside space, make it count by giving it a valuable function. A café-style table and chairs are all that's required as a sweet spot to enjoy meals or coffee. The galvanized steel mailbox and the sweet wee watering can, as planters, gently allude to the metal wall detail that awaits inside.

2. They say that "every dog has its day"—and thanks to an old farm sink, repurposed as a canine wash station, every dog can have its bath, too.

unique heritage) is wildly appealing and important when creating a memorable escape. This beautiful home is the perfect case in point, in that the surrounding houses are of similar age. Neither the passage of time nor the river's erosive drive has undermined this joyous pocket. As such, the property, and its neighbours, feel protected and preserved as part of quintessential "Olde England."

From experience, we've observed that one of the keys to a successful retreat is starting the escapist journey long before the front door's threshold has been crossed. Here, for example, access to the house is over an old humpback bridge which affords a first glimpse of the Cotswold structure, an edifice that seems to glow thanks to the nature of the stone, a yellow, fossil-rich Jurassic limestone.

Many of those who escape the city do so to get closer to nature, and for Mouse Martin, this was a driving factor. During spring and summer months, the banks are covered in daisies and wildflowers, the old sycamore tree in the garden bows into the river and an abundance of wildlife can be seen when sitting outside on the porch. River voles, kingfishers, frogs, trout, heron and ducks congregate to join visitors who choose to sit on the doorstep and listen to the river trickling by. It's like a traffic jam of nature... only much more enjoyable.

It was Audrey Hepburn who famously said: "To plant a garden is to believe in tomorrow," and in this garden, her poignant words resonate. Walking around the peaceful setting, there's a sense of permanence and growth. And, in that regard, relaxed and rewarding "tomorrows" seem somehow guaranteed.

So any hurdles as the project endured? Martin explains that tackling an older property such as hers requires considerable liaising with local planners, who want to retain the area's original charm whilst allowing homeowners the opportunity to transform unused buildings into amazing spaces.

Her renovation was actually pretty straightforward, although she had to build retaining walls to protect the house against water erosion and the garden from flooding. By using old stone to mimic the barn, the walls amply serve their purpose whilst appearing to have been there for centuries. It's a valuable lesson in using sympathetic mediums to maintain the property's original vernacular.

So what makes this cottage so special? For us it's the fact that, whilst creating a comfortable and rewarding retreat, its owner displays a deft touch when it comes to preserving original features. English country style personified, the look is beautifully "lived in," with elements like distressed timber, stone and worn linen merging to create a natural, friendly colour palette.

The inherent detail is stunning—timber beams have been exposed; plaster is stripped back to reveal the beauty of restored, original stonework. But of course it's all about the mix: newer elements add counterbalance and pedigree—French doors in the living zone, for example, "frame" the garden and allow fresh breezes to waft through on warm evenings. And then there's that wood burner, around which guests can gather as the mercury dips…

Martin's decorative sensibility proves it isn't necessary to spend a huge amount of money to achieve commanding results. Less can be more (in terms of spend and actual objects

1. Ah, yes; the touchy-feely quotient. Texture is your best friend with this look. This in mind, intersperse worn timber pieces with heavy-weave linen and rough matting to complement the 3D nature of the beams and exposed stone detail. And feel relaxed as smooth areas such as flat walls and painted flooring provide breathing space and airy punctuation.

2. Reclaim the past and bring it into the future—top old industrial mechanisms with cast-off doors to create a unique heritage table like this one. In this day and age, there's a real liberation with interior design. If your creation makes you happy, and if your vision—however strange it may seem to others—satisfies the purpose for which it was intended, then job done: that's what a good interior should be all about.

3. Let a builder's yard become your designer outlet: the corrugated-steel panels and reclaimed lumber moderate costs, whilst solidifying overall style credentials. The trick to making older buildings appear "younger" is to be quirky: specify unusual elements, but opt for inventory that appears worn and loved, just like the building itself. For us, it all comes down to atmosphere and the creation, by schematic layering, thereof.

4. A reclaimed farmhouse sink is serviced by pipe fittings and outdoor taps fashioned into a unique washing station. Elements like this provide schematic levity: we applaud the creation of anything that's a little left of centre. Google "architectural salvage" to find your nearest suppliers of interesting decorative assets.

or finishes) as long as what is there is carefully curated to create a singular, rewarding experience. Every item, it seems, was chosen to enhance and equip the unique escape. Interspersing handmade pieces with upcycled items creates a lived-in and loved environment that's all about making guests feel relaxed at every turn.

Where possible, things from the past have been reborn as inspired items. An old clothes mangle is reworked as a table, old fire buckets become industrial lampshades and vintage doors are dramatically reinterpreted as kitchen cupboards and even a bed head. And there's more: silver forks are reborn as coat hooks, grain sacks as curtains and scaffolding planks as counters in the kitchen. Nothing is surplus—in small spaces, everything must count, right?

Ah, yes, that kitchen. The "heart of the home" analogy has seldom been more pertinent than in Filly Island's food-prep zone. Here the heart beats hard, thanks to textural corrugated

steel-wall cladding, tempered with worn timber and vintage accessories that elicit a standout space that draws visitors like a magnet.

The upcycle story continues in the bathroom, where a red-painted claw-foot bath is like lipstick on an already beautiful face, and in the bedroom courtesy of stripped timber, grain sacks and restored second-hand radiators, which suffuse the space with a softly vintage vibe.

For all its inclusions, however, this home doesn't feel in any way cluttered: it simply feels eclectic. Whilst some observers might describe this style as shabby chic, we'd suggest there's nothing even remotely shabby about the space. Yet it certainly displays its chic credentials with style that's as English as cricket, and just as capable of bowling you over.

1. The barn's history is afforded a casual nod thanks to the reclaimed door that hangs on a barn-door sliding mechanism. The old door looks great, and the sliding steel mechanism changes the door's orientation from "swing" to "roll." (DIY outlets carry the requisite parts, for which you'll pay between $100 and $200.) Hey, it's classic two-for-one: super stylish and a smart space-saver in one bargain. What's not to like?

2. Using a reclaimed door—hung on its original hinges—as a bed head is an easy DIY, and an affordable way of adding a spot of vintage atmosphere. Jump online, search "reclaimed doors" and expect to pay between $50 and $100 for suitable time-travelled portals.

3. GET NAKED! Spell out the good times with quirky artwork that makes you smile. Experiment with self-adhesive letters on sections of wood or canvas, or freestyle with acrylic paint and artist's brushes to tailor individual pieces to suit your own style.

4. Here, a large, unbroken wall has been covered with a huge map of the local area, with a pin showing the precise location of this wee escape. And when it comes to making a bold statement, a little goes a long, long way: a pint of paint brings this salvaged tub to life.

While the building appears to levitate over the softly undulating rock, it doesn't dominate the landscape: the green roof and verdant planting ensure this, for the most part obscuring the structure's lines, softening its visual impact and allowing it to recede into the background. Nature, as we see it, remains the strongest visual element.

Go Home Bay

LOCATION
Georgian Bay,
Ontario, Canada

COMPLETION YEAR
2013

OWNERS
Ian MacDonald and
Diane MacDiarmid

ARCHITECT
Ian MacDonald
Architect

CONTRACTOR
Darlington
Construction

SIZE
1,400 sf (130 sqm)

NOTABLE BUILDING MATERIALS
Wood-framed superstructure clad in
cedar shingle, steel-framed floor infilled
with Structural Insulated Panels (SIPS),
to minimize contact with the whaleback
rock outcrop upon which it sits

UTILITIES
Electricity (on-grid supply), heating
(wood stoves throughout with back-up
auxiliary electric heating), water
(drinking water filtered from the lake),
waste (septic system)

PHOTOGRAPHY
Tom Arban

Whilst we might typically associate stealth technology—which provides invisible shielding—with the army, warships, fighter planes and James Bond, the notion of stealth can also be applied in other contexts. In architecture, for example—via the work, notably, of Canadian Ian MacDonald, whose "Go Home Bay" cabin disappears into the landscape, providing sublime anonymity for the highly regarded creative and his family.

Situated on a fifteen-acre parcel on Georgian Bay—an area immortalized by Canada's celebrated Group of Seven painters—the modern cabin is virtually undetectable from the water. To further enhance its invisibility, MacDonald chose to install a living roof, which, aside from its camouflaging qualities, enables an irrigation system which floods the overhead organic membrane, as required, to cool the living quarters below.

The creation of the intimate four-season family cabin is the realization of a thoughtful and deeply personal appraisal of the cultural heritage—and landscape—of Ontario's Georgian Bay archipelago. The area's unique topography sees legions of small, rocky islands topped by scraggly white pines shaped by the west winds, a raw beauty which has remained unchanged—for the most part, certainly—since the dawn of time.

The area's popularity, however, has seen the landscape vulnerable to development, with many over-scaled structures dwarfing their surroundings and disturbing the natural realm. In this "bigger is better" mindset, homeowners are prone to architectural ostentation, but not so the sensitive visionary Ian MacDonald, nor his uncomplicated residential masterpiece.

As we see it, the element of surprise serves to make any cabin experience memorable: schematic elements confound expectation to awaken the senses and make project "interaction" unexpectedly exciting.

Sometimes it'll be a steep roof pitch flying at a forty-five-degree angle across a tapestry of otherwise perpendicular lines, or a sightline to a beautiful vista that's hidden from view through other elevations. Perhaps a building material that breaks the

2. The adjustable exterior panels can be used to screen the room from the sun and create shade. In the background, at the entrance, cedar shingles create a wall that's guaranteed to be a textural talking point.

tempo of everything else. Or simply a paint colour which mightn't be expected as part of the overall picture.

The primary element of surprise here, though, is the way in which MacDonald has strategically positioned his structure to respect the beautiful shoreline which stirs a sense of anticipation upon arrival. When visitors approach by water (following a sixteen-mile journey from the nearest dock), native oak, elm and white blossom trees disguise the building, yielding only brief glimpses (a flash of glass, perhaps, or a whisper of steel through branches) that whet the appetite.

Climbing from the dock through the dense juniper meadow, surrounded by tall white pines, anticipation builds as visitors encounter a low-level, charcoal-toned "box" that appears to float, thanks to its partially cantilevered nature. It's a commanding edifice, yet it only hints at the joys that lie ahead.

Entering into a simple vestibule, vast views and expansive spaces are blinkered (in part by a stunning wall of jet-painted cedar shingles—unusual, but interesting, in the context of an interior), as if to prepare onlookers for their transition into the long galley kitchen, a space that doubles as a windowed corridor to the cabin's rear compartments.

1

Back there, a cozy sitting area swathed in sheepskin is serviced by a wood stove and views to forest behind the house. In the adjacent living room, more than forty linear feet of fenestration views down and across the Go Home Bay channel. Sunshades integrated within the cabin's envelope reduce heat gain, and the main space, capped by operable clerestories, transforms into a screened-in porch with lift and slide doors to improve cross-ventilation.

A concrete wall provides a metropolitan focal point and a warming heat source when the mercury dips. The marriage of concrete, timber, glass and statement furniture is a joy to behold, these conspiring elements serving up solid atmosphere and a veritable cocoon-like feel. It's a place where MacDonald

1. A beautiful three-quarter-height concrete wall separates the living space from the hallway whilst allowing light to pass between both zones. In winter, the concrete retains heat provided by two wood-burning stoves, and, accordingly, rooms stay warmer for longer. Glass, on three sides, surrounds the compartment with greenery, whilst creating a sense of infinity in this already-spacious environment.

2. Large-scale windows immerse occupants in nature, blurring boundaries between indoors and out. The long, lean sofa and dining table follow the stretched rectangular proportions of the room, whilst glass railings on the deck provide safety with minimal obstruction to views.

1. Creating bedrooms sufficiently large for more than one function works particularly well in the cabin context, especially since second homes, generally speaking, are smaller than their occupants' principal homes. To this end, adding a chair and bookshelves creates a useful library nook with amazing bay views. Escaping the city is one thing; but escaping to a private corner in your retreat furthers the indulgent journey.

2. The specification of custom furnishings ensures that everything fits the space for which it was intended.

balances his professional remit with the call of the wild. A place, he explains, where purest decompression and recharge occur, far from the fast-spinning cogs of his urban existence. It's fair to describe it as surprisingly cozy, for all its modernity. In short, it simply works.

Getting his creation to this point, however, was far from relaxing, as MacDonald explains. The logistical issues of assembling and building this manicured vision in a remote, water-access-only area proved problematic; but teamwork, to employ the old cliché, made the dream work.

Careful timetabling with trusted contractors and suppliers allayed issues before they burgeoned. Most construction materials were coordinated onto a single barge to reduce the embodied energy of transportation, with certain larger components (such as the joists and framework) dropped in by helicopter.

Starting late in the season, a highly organized effort got the floor frame in place before winter, so that the superstructure could be erected as soon as the bay became frozen. For once, the barometric shift and biting climate proved allies: access over the ice (by snowmobile) made everything substantially easier.

With its roots in cabins of the past (yet with modernistic leanings that reference the future), MacDonald's cabin is a boiled-down amalgam of everything that's important in a retreat. Sixteen miles from the nearest dock and positioned to complement (rather than compete with) nature, being stealthy, not showy, results in a retreat that feels for all the world like a succulent, homely secret simply waiting to be shared.

The steel cladding's vertical lines make
the structure appear taller, whilst echoing
the lean trunks of the surrounding trees.

Grand-Pic Chalet

LOCATION	**SIZE**
Austin, Quebec, Canada	1,460 sf (136 sqm)
COMPLETION YEAR	**NOTABLE BUILDING MATERIALS**
2017	Corrugated steel cladding, steel roof with birch panelling
OWNERS	
Clients of APPAREIL Architecture	**UTILITIES**
	On-grid supply with electric underfloor heating
ARCHITECT	
APPAREIL Architecture	**PHOTOGRAPHY**
	Félix Michaud
CONTRACTOR	
Martin Coley Construction	

In cabin design, when simplicity is proficiently mastered, the smallest things become much more interesting. Aspects such as colour selections, for example, find their relevance suddenly elevated when fewer "supporting cast" layers are in play.

Think about a large box, topped with a large lid, and imagine the darkness contained therein. Then imagine flipping that sombre palette to the exterior and transferring the light quotient within. That's exactly what's happened at Grand-Pic Chalet, a two-bedroom, two-floor, two-structure holiday respite that's externally attired in black metal, but layered with bright timber cladding across its internal elevations.

Working to the client brief (that being to distill the essence of "cabin" and create a space that contained only essentials), APPAREIL architects were inspired by the surrounding forest, peaks and flatlands (not to mention Lake Memphremagog—a freshwater glacial waterway that spans the U.S. and Canada) as their pared-back vision developed.

"Before properly imagining the project," explains APPAREIL's founder Kim Pariseau, "we were guided by the terrain's characteristics." The surrounding topography greatly influenced the project's layout, with parking, for example, situated on the periphery of the land parcel so as not to distract from the cabin's uncomplicated nature.

Furthermore, the rustic pathway leading to the residence cuts through the trees with minimal disruption, eventually yielding to cedar decking as it encounters the property. Remarkably for such a boxy, contemporary structure, it doesn't feel in any way ill at ease in its surroundings. Quite the contrary, in fact: it sits comfortably against the purity of the landscape.

Grand-Pic Chalet is made up of two structural compartments—one large and one small—both of which are dressed in shiny black corrugated steel, set under sombre steel roofing. Observing the elevation, the TV show *Twin Peaks* comes to mind, courtesy of the ominous, gabled structures whose dark

2. The naive yet familiar house structures blend seamlessly into the environment.

3. Both structures boast similar gabled form and, although not joined, they read as one thanks to shared finishes.

4. Darkly attired homes disappear into the background, leaving the environment to make the bolder statement.

5. The black-on-black outdoor shower provides an invisible source of refreshing water.

ridge-lines point skyward, evoking intrigue akin to the most mysterious episodes of David Lynch's cult series.

The house's primary living quarters are contained within the larger of the peaked boxes, a two-bedroom retreat that houses an open-concept living, dining and kitchen space. The smaller structure accommodates additional storage, whilst acting as a privacy screen to a private deck with an outdoor shower.

Fashioned from Western red cedar, the deck snakes around the main house, providing a home for entertaining and outdoor grilling. Meanwhile, the naturally silvered cedar provides a colour link between the building's black sheet steel and the timbers of the forest. There's a confident vibe, with each

1. Vertical strips of white panelling clad the exterior wall of the second floor, effectively strengthening the shape's outline and creating a house-within-a-house look.

2. The grey cedar walkway provides a simple bridge between the structures.

3. Windowless across certain elevations, the mini-compound has an industrial feel that belies the warm, birch-clad welcome that waits within.

building serving up differently scaled shadows as the sun moves across the day to illuminate the changing relationship of both structures.

Standing at the doorway, bridging inside and out, is where we're most aware of the aforementioned colour contrast: black-framed openings offer captivating glimpses across the streamlined black, concrete, birch and white scheme. The interior landscape showcases what happens when unnecessary inclusions are minimized to allow an unbridled marriage of colour and shape to prevail.

By using the same bright cladding throughout (and for the built-in storage units), walls are visually "undisturbed," making the space appear larger and more open. Light pours in from the huge window configuration to further uplift mood and connect dwellers to the beautiful outside vistas.

Indeed, it's that connection to the outside that's so important when it comes to creating any forest dwelling, not least this one. And nothing connects better than walls of glass.

Here, the proximity of the surrounding forest fills the windows, creating a decorative backdrop whilst literally enveloping occupants in nature. Man-made and organic play beautifully

here: even the long, lean lines of the trees outside are echoed in the soaring nature of the window frames and courtesy of the stretched lines of the wood-stove chimney.

"The owners," explains Pariseau, "wanted a warm but bright space, to host family and friends in perfect harmony with the environment." Observing the cabin, it's abundantly clear their ambitions were satisfied. "The realization of all of that," she concludes, "is a restrained, yet at once welcoming space, one that breathes, free of visual or ergonomic congestion, wherever possible."

In the tightly tailored kitchen, cabinets and countertops are white, whilst the hanging lamps, faucet, bar stools and dining chairs are jet—the marriage serving up tonal contrast as viewed against a backdrop of birch. Once again, simplicity is key, the cabin's aesthetic cleverly assembled to offer little more than life's bare essentials.

1. Storage and mechanicals are located behind the kitchen. Housing these elements in one zone keeps other areas free from pipes and meters.

2. Pared-back finishes create an almost monastic tranquility.

3. The fridge resides in a separate pantry, thereby keeping the kitchen elevation free from the punctuation of appliances. White quartz countertops sit atop the white panelled island to create a single white "block." This aesthetic is fortified by a black faucet, sink, stools and lighting.

But come on: there's a luxury in the purity of "less" that's beyond compelling, right? How often have you seen a potentially beautiful space overwhelmed by an inventory of disassociated clutter and unnecessary furniture? It was textile designer and novelist William Morris, of the British Arts and Crafts movement, who said: "Have nothing in your house that you do not know to be useful, or believe to be beautiful." His words, written in the mid-nineteenth century, remain as relevant today as they were back then. Modernized, they read like this: "Get rid of all the crap." Take note.

Languidly spread across the lounge area, a large, upholstered grey sectional chesterfield maps out the room's footprint, carefully positioned to open up and greet the wood-burning fireplace in front of the window: a modernist, yet cozy, corner.

The second storey takes up half the area of the ground floor, galleried to create soaring ceilings which amplify the overall

feeling of space. There's a bathroom, and a pair of rooms, one of which is dressed as a "traditional" bedroom, and the other as a modern dormitory with two bed nooks, mirrored through a dividing wall.

We really like this cabin. In fact, we'd go as far as to say we love it. Its prevailing aesthetic, whilst uncomplicated, is so inviting. Reminded by Pariseau that her clients wanted an escape to simplify their existence, it's clear their wish was granted.

This is a sweet wee world where the machinations of work are left at the front door. The environment is all about communing with nature: it's pure, it's simple and it's uncomplicated, woven only with life's basic essentials, far from the cut and thrust of city life.

So what do *you* need to escape? Which trappings? Perhaps the answer is significantly simpler than you might think.

1. The rectangular lines of the sofa, table and built-in storage units flow with the building to create solidarity and strength. Spaces feel larger when free of clutter, and having less "stuff" allows you to enjoy what you do have for its singular beauty.

2. A simple colour palette—concrete, birch and black—is used throughout to proffer a cohesive, singular identity.

We love entertaining and very much enjoy
having people visit, but of course some
guests like their own space. And so, as much
as we were delighted with the extended scale
of Grey Gardens, we decided that, for invitees
who enjoy a little more privacy, a separate
guest annex was a smart idea.

Grey Gardens

LOCATION
Drag Lake, Ontario,
Canada

COMPLETION YEAR
2014

OWNERS
Colin McAllister and
Justin Ryan

ARCHITECTS
Jodanne Aggett,
Haliburton Timber Mart
(main cottage), Discovery
Dream Homes (sunroom)

INTERIOR DESIGNERS
Colin McAllister and
Justin Ryan

CONTRACTOR
Randy Blain Construction

SIZE
1,750 sf (163 sqm), plus a
385-sf (36-sqm) modular
prefabricated bunkie

NOTABLE BUILDING MATERIALS
Stick-built, sided in grey-painted
Cape Cod cedar and set under a black
shingle roof, engineered oak flooring;
screened porch is cedar post-and-
beam construction with Sunspace
Sunrooms window system, custom
windows by euro + glasshaus

UTILITIES
Electricity (on-grid supply), heating
(baseboards), water (well water),
waste (septic system)

PHOTOGRAPHY
Brandon Barré (interiors),
Bob Newnham (exterior)

From the moment we spotted the "for sale" sign outside our
diamond-in-the-rough "slanty shanty" at Bonham Bay, Ontario,
we knew we had to own it. We've always been boys, you see, who
enjoy a furtive dalliance with the underdog, so we held our collective breath and made an appointment to view the sad wee
shack. And we fell instantly in love.

Positioned atop a one-acre plot about sixty feet from the
shoreline, the cottage was in a desperate state. Uninhabited for
the best part of two years, Mother Nature had crawled her way
into every corner, delivering, with unstinting dedication, an
arsenal of water ingress, rot and mold.

But oh, that potential. Built on piers which were buckled and
crumbling in several places—causing the cabin to lean to one

1. In one corner, an $80 Craigslist swing chair is a schematic foil to the Indonesian live-edge table, whilst Wishbone chairs layer in restrained mood courtesy of their black frames and blond raffia seat-pads.

2. Why does this space work so well? Because there's so much to see, and so many places for the eye to go. The tan-hide sofa provides visual and ergonomic softening, whilst the Stûv log-burning stove adds a thoroughly modern touch. Take it from us: for such a small contraption, it works remarkably well. The fireplace throws out intense heat from a drum-shaped directional firebox that twists on its lower axis to deliver warmth in various directions, as and when required.

side and the windows to jam shut—the spatial volume had us captivated from the get-go. Okay, so it was utterly ramshackle, but we could fix all that. It's what we do, right? Cottage salvation, after all, is our stock in decorative trade.

The living and dining areas were generous, and the loft bedroom (albeit spoiled by lowered ceilings and space-consuming side walls) reeked of opportunity. We immediately envisioned a slick, urban reversion with acres of white drywall married with walnut-toned ceilings and myriad mid-century layers. Oak flooring, toffee-coloured leather sofas, gnarled-wood bed frames and live-edged detailing would seal the deal and, in doing so, compose a stylistically modern vibe.

Anyway, as we've found with real estate over and over again, the early bird catches the first worm. Knowing that another buyer was also pursuing the sad wee cabin, we made a successful bid—at asking—and took possession just four weeks later.

Okay, so we could have delayed proceedings by offering a few grand less, but the opportunity to champion the project could

so easily have been seized by the other party. If you're not *fast*, you're *last*.

Taking possession, we were little short of thrilled: we knew we'd enjoy living there. This observed, it's fair to suggest we always have one eye trained on future value, and whilst (at the time) we had no plans to sell the cottage, we wanted it "market-ready" when the moment eventually arrived.

Discussions with our realtor made us realize the cottage was a little on the small side to meet future market expectations head-on, so we dialogued with the local planning department to assess the viability of "lifting" the cottage and adding a base-ment floor. Our vision, thankfully, was approved, without rever-sion, and we were able to progress without delay.

Lifting the whole cottage? Yes, in its entirety. Having worked, previously, with a company in whose standards we firmly believed, we invited them to appraise the project. And whilst it

1. In many parts of cottage country, entomological invasion can be unbearable, especially from May until August when blackflies and mosquitoes are at their worst. It's therefore commonplace for many North American retreats to have a screened porch, and so, in association with Discovery Dream Homes and Sunspace Sunrooms, we built an A-frame outdoor lounge adjacent to the dining room. Constructed from Western red cedar post and beams, the vaulted-ceiling space creates an immediate sense of scale, even though it measures just 275 sf (26 sqm).

2

2. The aluminum-framed window system allows air to pass through mesh bug screens, with adjustable clear vinyl panels to keep out rain and snow. The doors are on a folding track system, which allows them to concertina open.

might sound unlikely that an entire house can be lifted off the ground, that's precisely what happened.

First up, large, square holes were excavated at ground level at each of the cabin's four corners, and reinforced steel beams were run along the building's underside. A mechanical frame, thereafter, was positioned below the beams, at which point the apparatus was lifted, taking the cottage with it, inch by inch.

Every foot or so, wooden posts were inserted underneath (think Jurassic-scaled Jenga or Lincoln Logs) until the structure was literally floating fifteen feet above ground. This done, our contractors built a cinder-block perimeter wall, with openings for windows and patio doors, and formed a floor with self-levelling concrete.

After several days, when the concrete had set, the cottage was lowered back onto the new perimeter wall and presto: the biggest part of the basement addition was complete. Thereafter, it

was simply a matter of forming the room spaces and inserting a staircase to connect the lower level to the other floors.

Next order of business was the addition of a "shed" dormer (which projects beyond the original line of the roof to amplify floor and head-space within) on the mezzanine floor. Building this provided more space for a generously scaled bathroom, an asset the cottage sorely missed. Sure, there was already a small bathroom on the main floor, but our plan being to turn the cottage into a luxurious waterside retreat with all modern conveniences, we needed substantially better facilities.

Extending the bedroom roofline by forty-five degrees—beyond its original pitch—allowed us to add a generous bathroom, into which we installed a hefty stone sink set on a steel base, as well as a toilet and a shower compartment.

With washroom activities discreetly hidden behind barnboard portals, the resultant space is fresh and welcoming:

1. Removing the lowered ceiling and side walls maximized space. Cladding, thereafter, with walnut-stained cedar delivered extra character: we love the subdued mood with which the room is suffused.

In keeping with the loft vibe (hello, condo at the lake?), we added a hefty, brushed-steel bed (note how the wood inlay adds visual and literal texture), timber-topped nightstands and a wall of barnboard doors that roll silently across the entranceway to the ensuite. The tricked-out vibe is modern but friendly, thanks to layers of faux fur and woolen throws and a scattering of plump, yielding cushions. Oh, and witness how pops of red add a spot of drama. Just a little, right? It's all you need.

2. If you follow our work, you'll know we love trawling antique barns and thrift stores for items to upcycle. An example of this are the ten-buck shoe molds which we sanded, sprayed black and arranged in a neat row as towel storage. Our maxim? It's not what you have, but what you do with it that makes the biggest difference.

3. We specified flush-mounted pot lights and energy-efficient radiant (underfloor) heating. Graphite marble tile offers an indulgent feel, whilst dreamy ebony-toned faucets and storage niches are cute finishing details. We opted for a long, steel-framed vanity which, topped with a custom black tap, oozes "modern cottage."

4. To serve as a vanity below the new window, we cut live-edged hemlock into a tapered wedge and crowned it with a stone basin. Further visual softening comes from the wood-topped stool and the naturally shed antler found in the nearby forest. Details, right?

precisely what the doctor ordered to improve real estate value and, indeed, daily lifestyle.

Downstairs, large rolling patio doors and huge windows were a simple masterstroke: with such fantastic landscape—and undeniably beautiful lake views—to have installed anything less would have been to serve the project a huge injustice. And boy—do those badass doors let light flood in.

Ah, yes, that beautiful natural illumination, light which reflects perfectly as a partner to the unfussy walls. But hold it: white-painted drywall? At the cabin? When we advised our contractor that we planned a snowy palette, he was initially surprised; but our logic was simple: we wanted bags of schematic contrast.

Unlike our Muskoka log cabin, for example, this project was less about "woodsy" atmosphere, and more about delivering the crisp, mid-century vibe which we believed the space could so easily accommodate.

1–2. Open plan, to the max. The A-frame is essentially one big sharing space with blurred boundaries between living, dining and kitchen. The glass and metal bannister system, by Sunspace Sunrooms, simplifies the staircase elevation and ensures it doesn't dominate the open plan space.

With fenestration and portals successfully addressed, we added wood flooring throughout. In most cabins, engineered boards are a more sensible solution than solid lumber: their structural integrity deals better with the vagaries of temperature and moisture fluctuation. We also included a simple kitchen with built-in refrigeration and a deep sink.

A peninsula, topped with concrete-look quartz, forms a neat breakfast bar that contains a built-in stove and a dishwasher tucked neatly out of sight. It mightn't be an overly large space, but we certainly crammed in loads of user-friendly function.

Completed, the style of this cottage more than references our affection for contemporary rustic meets mid-century modern. Okay—so, in isolation, each vibe is very different from the other—but their strength is in their combination. Little wonder, then, we so enjoyed our time in Grey Gardens. And little wonder we borrowed several of its component aspects during subsequent projects.

1–2. Working to our plan, the structure was built off-site by an independent contractor and, upon completion, trucked to site and craned atop concrete piers. Measuring just 220 sf (20 sqm), it's a compact prospect, designed to contain a full (albeit tiny) three-piece bathroom, a four-bedded bunk room, and an ancillary dining nook.

3. Prior to its arrival, we built perimeter piers (upon which the bunkie sits), added power lines and established a connection to the property's main sewer. Sided and roofed to match the cottage, the bunkie is a fun little structure that guests love. The best bit? It arrived on the back of a flat-bed truck fully assembled (and even fully decorated). The perfect finishing touch to Grey Gardens.

DESIGN
YOUR ESCAPE

Closeness (and connection) to nature, awareness of changing seasons, enjoying relaxing spaces and sharing real-life experiences are the very backbone of cabin lifestyle. But of course owning a retreat is about so much more than simply existing in a building. It's about family. It's a calming thought as warm breath escapes on a cold breeze. It's a roaring fire that provides protection from the storm. It's maple syrup poured over stacks of hot, steaming pancakes. It's lazy days on the dock drinking locally sourced beer whilst the sun goes down. *Ah*, it's bliss. *Pure*, unadulterated bliss.

So much more than simply bricks and mortar, lumber and stone, the cabin is a template upon which to layer life's finer aspects with friends and family. Envision quiet nooks in which to relax and feel safe. Dream of that ideal spot in which to tell a story… or whisper a secret. A well-planned escape should bring out the best in everyone who visits and inspire them to share good times and make sweet, enduring memories. Say, aren't we only on this planet for a short time? Yes? So let's make it a good time. In fact, let's make it a *great* time…

We'll forever remember a trip we made to the beautiful Wickaninnish Inn resort in Tofino, British Columbia. The smart-thinking owners (who clearly subscribe to the mantra "Find a fault, make a feature") have successfully turned their rainy, windy, quiet period into "storm season." Theirs, in fact, was a masterstroke of rebranding and learning to look at things differently. As word has travelled, storm season has become one of their *busiest* periods, with people flocking to embrace the grey-scale landscape, the crashing seas and the wild winds that relentlessly batter the coastline. They crawl Chesterman Beach wrapped in weather-baffling clothes. And then gather around fires in the hotel to chat about their adventures whilst savouring the best of local food and wine. Seriously: it's *amazing*.

Recognizing the emotional benefits of owning (or indeed renting) a rural retreat—and allowing that to have a positive effect on your mindset—is a crucial part of embracing the cabin lifestyle. About *so* much more than simply "style and surface," the cabin experience provides an opportunity to make daily changes that will enhance your overall well-being. Out of the city, it's easier to simplify life's existence and look at things in a substantially more positive manner. And if you can *see* the best, you can *be* the best. It just takes a little time.

The cabin is a template upon which to layer life's finer aspects with friends and family.

MAKE A
READING LIST

Block out the colder months, or embrace the sunshine, by getting your bookworm on. Revisiting a favourite tome in your comfy wee reading nook is like being reacquainted with an old friend. Hey, these days you can even buy reading socks in bookstores to amplify the comfort quotient as you get lost in those wonderful words. Write out a reading list in your journal, adjusting content to suit the seasons, and see how many stories you can get through each year.

RESTAURANT
AT-HOME

Reach out to friends and family and invite them around, with the emphasis on small cozy gatherings rather than huge, formal dinners. Potluck dinners are super fun. Prepare simple meals with great ingredients and encourage your guests to share in the experience. Alternatively, enjoy "self-cook" food with a Korean hot stone or prepare fondue or raclette. Gathered around the table as you jostle for space, it's a great bonding experience, and a great way to spend time.

RELAX IN
THE KITCHEN

The slow food movement embraces dishes that fly in the face of fast food, an ethos that's particularly at home in the cabin context where clocks run (deliberately) slow. It's all about gastronomy that takes time, so break out the slow cooker and start planning those pot roasts. Baking, too, is highly rewarding, and *oh*, that tasty outcome. Reach for a mixer and start turning out bread, scones and banana loaves that can be gifted to, or shared with, others.

BECOME A
RURAL STARBUCKS

Everyone loves coffee. It's no coincidence there are coffee shops on street corners *everywhere* and, like a hug in a cup, there's no better way to start the day or warm up during colder times. Choose a great coffee maker, research delicious bean variants and invest in some handmade mugs from a local potter to make that previously humble hot drink an escapist experience.

DISCONNECT
TO RECONNECT

Turn off the phone, leave the laptop at home and tether your tablet in another room. The demanding call of modern life creates pressure to be available and connected at all times, leaving less opportunity to garner your thoughts and enjoy some downtime. It took us two years to install high-speed Internet at our cabin, yet we somehow survived.

GET OUT
OF THE CITY

Don't limit vacation time to warmer months; make a point of escaping the city during winter, too, to experience a quiet rural life you perhaps didn't know existed. We drive three hours north to enjoy frozen lakes, dog sleighs and snow-dusted forests that look for all the world like scenes from classic Christmas cards. It's totally escapist, *thoroughly* rewarding and reminds us that simple things can add up to unbridled magnificence.

The Monument Channel cottage is completely self-sufficient. Powered by solar panels, it uses its own water filtration system, and its own sewage treatment plant. Who said that no man (or woman) is an island?

Monument Channel Cottage

LOCATION
Monument Channel,
Ontario, Canada

COMPLETION YEAR
2013

OWNERS
Charles and Robin Gane

ARCHITECT
CORE Architects

CONTRACTOR
Cove Construction

SIZE
2,125 sf (197 sqm)

NOTABLE BUILDING MATERIALS
Douglas fir, glass, ipe, local stone

UTILITIES
Electricity (solar panels), heating
(solar), water (its own water filtration
system), waste (its own sewage
treatment plant)

PHOTOGRAPHY
Paul Orenstein

When it comes to ambition, some people take slow, tentative steps towards greatness, whilst other players march swiftly towards victory, with apparently unstinting ability to make good decisions. One such visionary, soundly occupying the latter category, is Toronto-based architect Charles Gane who, along with his wife Robin, purchased a water access–only property on Ontario's Georgian Bay.

To get the lay of the land, Charles and Robin, together with their children, spent a first summer dodging rattlesnakes, cooking alfresco and sleeping under canvas, during which time they developed a feel for the softly undulating granite, the changing light and the remarkable topography as it transitioned from season to season. This unique treasure trove of inspiration clearly inflected Charles's vision and assisted in the journey from drawing board to the grand respite his family now call their (home from) home.

But of course, the build was anything but easy. Given the remote nature of the cottage, all materials had to be barged in.

When you're working on the mainland and suddenly need an ancillary component, it's easy to grab what you need, right? But when your project is water access, the rules are different: you can't simply dash to a supplier on a whim. Organization, ahead of time, is paramount.

The predominant building material is a lumber genus that features heavily throughout. From the exposed post-and-beam structure to wall finishes to interior cabinetry and the impressive kitchen island, it's all Douglas fir, a solid and dependable genus beloved of the architectural community.

Exterior cladding is either wood plank or cedar shingles, with hard-wearing Brazilian ipe used for decking and for the guardrail that appears to float atop the perimeter glass railings.

It truly is a *remarkable* home, a breathtaking mix of timber, stone and glass which somehow, for all its modernity, recedes quietly into the Georgian Bay topography.

1 . The huge and undeniably impressive eighteen-foot kitchen island offers multiple preparation and seating areas, and serves as a stunning focal point that's functional and beautiful in equal measure. By day, the space is flooded with natural illumination via walls of fenestration (and courtesy of the ceiling windows above) whereas by night it's illuminated thanks to galvanised steel pendants that infuse the eating area with an edgy, industrial vibe.

2. The commodious, flowing space delivers multiple nooks to which users can retreat should they wish to be alone with their thoughts, as well as a huge sharing space that's all about congregation and bringing people together. This for us is the very essence of a successful retreat.

Entering, there's an immediate sense of scale courtesy of an open-shelved kitchen which groans with *objets trouvés*, crockery and glassware. The extra-wide kitchen island yields first to the dining area and then towards a cozy living area centred around a stone-fronted hearth.

In our experience, large, open-concept spaces can feel unfocused, even sterile, but Charles avoided any such worry by suffusing his cottage with an overall sense of comfort via indulgent wood finishes, textural layers and a series of inviting nooks.

These relaxation "pockets" are the perfect place in which to enjoy music or simply tuck away with a magazine or a good book. With several nooks around the cottage, occupants can move with the sun—or indeed the moon—and totally relax into the moment.

It might sound like extra work, but, when planning any project—whether it be a ground-up build or the reversion of an

1. Polished concrete floors in the kitchen and bathroom strengthen the overall look, and in doing so bring a metropolitan condominium aesthetic into the modern rustic space. It'll come as no surprise, then, to learn that Gane's professional remit regularly finds him engaged in the realization of urban tower blocks. By his own admission, he has brought elements of those construction projects to his weekend home.

1. Off the home's principal congregation space is an ancillary outdoor living room whose rectilinear shapes and architectural pattern mimic the home's interior. Long benches flank a rectangular coffee table, with the entire vignette arranged in front of a tall log fireplace with views around and beyond to the stunning landscape.

existing space—considering light, and how it travels around your home, is *critical*. The positioning of function (dining, seating, sleeping, etc.) should be carefully appraised so that space is allowed for harnessing natural illumination (or to deal with a shortage of same) as each day rolls forward.

Choosing to build *onto* the land—rather than blasting rock to accommodate the proposed structure—creates engagement between the terrain and the house: the ground floor's two principal compartments (the living area, as described, and the master bedroom suite, which lies to the rear) effectively straddle two rocks which are intersected, thereafter, by a "bridge" that creates a sheltered tunnel with sightlines in two directions to the great outdoors.

And it's that connection to the great outdoors that's so remarkable, as viewed through enormous windows—positioned throughout the entire building—which provide welcome cooling cross-breezes and a sublime sense of proportion.

Overall, for a building of such considerable scale, the atmosphere remains intimate, which, as we see it, comes down to the successful compartmentalization of the overall "box." Albeit open-concept, smart zoning at the hands of Gane blurs sightlines between each area. The kitchen, for example, whilst directly beside the principal fireside gathering area, delivers clear, purposeful boundaries thanks to its long counter, open-plan shelving and ample food storage tucked behind discreet pantry doors. As the kitchen runs along the glass-sided room, it's intersected, across its end elevation, by the living area, which runs from one side of the room to the other.

Gane's Monument Channel Cottage build is an architectural masterpiece. Sure, the landscape upon which the modern edifice sits is decidedly barren (Georgian Bay's blustery winds and softly undulating grey-scale rocky outcroppings assure that) but nestled behind the exterior's modern architectural vernacular, and shielded by acres of jet-framed fenestration, lies an inviting world where relaxation is catered to at every turn in an indulgent environment where comfort is forever king.

Like nature's spirit level, the long, lean lines
of this weekend retreat provide contrast to
the undulating landscape of Elgin Valley. And
in an area famous for fruit growing, barns
are commonplace, their vernacular instantly
relevant. As such, a weekend retreat like this
seems perfectly at ease amongst the orchards
and vineyards.

Old MacMommy

LOCATION
Elgin, Overberg,
South Africa

COMPLETION YEAR
2016

OWNERS
Clients of Scott +
Partners

ARCHITECT
Scott + Partners

CONTRACTOR
OJW Sustainable
Building and Joinery

SIZE
1,615 sf (150 sqm), plus additional
538 sf (50 sqm) deck-terrace

NOTABLE BUILDING MATERIALS
Steel-framed structure on a masonry
plinth, steel exterior cladding, spruce-
board internal surfaces for floors,
walls and ceiling, aluminum doors and
windows

UTILITIES
Electricity (solar powered with on-grid
back-up), water (on-grid supply and heat
pump), waste (septic system)

PHOTOGRAPHY
Greg Cox/Bureaux

Just an hour's drive from beautiful, bustling Cape Town sits Elgin Valley—the apple-growing region of South Africa. Flanked by undulating mountains and nature reserves, the protected orchards and cool climate make this area the perfect weekend escape from the city.

Who, after all, doesn't dream of a temperate environment, beautiful topography, and, of course, wine (lashings of it), conveniently positioned relatively close to home?

The owners, having worked and vacationed in Elgin Valley, had many friends nearby, a positive advantage when planning a holiday home. Whilst remote isolation suits some, we tend to choose pockets with pre-existing friends to ease passage into the wider community: there's a comfort in knowing that, should we ever need help in any regard, there are people to assist.

In dialogue with Cape Town architects Scott + Partners, the owners outlined their desire for a weekend bolthole that would simplify shared time and distill the idea of "holiday cabin" to its purest essence. In short, they dreamed a family retreat, with sufficient space for friends to visit. Simplicity, elegance and comfort would be watchwords, with an architectural vernacular designed to recede into the surrounding landscape.

And what a landscape it is. The cabin backs directly onto an orchard with breathtaking vistas of the beautiful mountain-scape, and stunning sunsets that paint the land in shimmering yellow tones as each day rounds out.

The architects endeavoured to ensure that "contact" with the landscape was always maintained, but the building site was on a steep slope (and adjacent to a dam) and presented certain challenges. By all accounts, it wasn't a typical, "make the walls

1. Transitioning from inside, the outdoor entertainment area is a seamless extension of the house and vista beyond.

2. Simplicity is strength—the combination of blond and black timber serves to create an uncluttered architectural vision.

3. A table that serves as an extension of the kitchen cabinetry reflects the duality of aesthetics and practicality: dining function remains close to food preparation, whilst the elevation's long lines magnify proportions.
The kitchen counter is made from brass, treated with heat to darken its surface and encourage aging—a process that continues with the passage of time.

disappear and create extensive decks and gardens" approach. Indeed, far from it ...

The topography dictated the creation of "moments," such as the deep window seats in the sitting room, walkways and master bedroom. These spots allow inhabitants to "pause" and connect with the outside without so much as stepping over the threshold.

"The element of surprise," explains the architect, "like turning a corner and being caught short by the light or by breathtaking views, never ceases to amaze." But none of this, of course, was happenstance. It was *all* exactly planned.

In conjunction with their clients, Scott + Partners settled on a contemporary barn aesthetic for practicality of construction, identifying that the proposed structure would cause minimal disturbance to the landscape. It's a very pure form that, even with modern punctures and apertures to welcome in light,

relates well to its context. Put simply, it looks perfectly at home in an orchard.

As well as being aesthetically justifiable in the rural context, barns, from our experience, are a practical and affordable way to build—important considerations in any environment, not least in remote areas such as Elgin Valley. And if elements can be created off-site, then all the better: the steel frame, for example, was made remotely, trucked in, and then erected on site before being enclosed and clad in corrugated sheeting.

The simplicity works incredibly well, creating a sense of space and an unbroken, focused appreciation of the surroundings. Inside, the interior cladding is 100 percent spruce, with pale timber walls and a pitched ceiling with clean lines that stay true to the barn's exterior silhouette. Punctuation from the soft-toned walls is delivered via mostly black-toned furnishings, lights, accessories and even the pots and pans in the kitchen. It's a monochromatic balancing act, but one that feels in no way forced or overplayed.

1. Uncomplicated form is a key ingredient in the main bedroom, where low-level custom beds (designed by architect Greg Scott) serve to visually increase ceiling height.

2. The steel ladder in this child's bedroom leads to an ancillary sleeping nook, the journey required to get there perpetuating the idea of "escape." Come on, who wouldn't want to climb a ladder and hide away with a good book?

3–4. Contrast is king, courtesy of white, smooth finishes set against rough, stacked-stone walls: this deliberate play of man-made and natural works well in homes that seek to merge the spirit of urban and country.

The monochrome journey is broken up, albeit briefly, by the freshly attired bathrooms that are predominantly rock-accented, with white finishes. The contrast of the huge, rough stones (excavated from the site) and the purity of the snowy floor works particularly well, especially when viewed through the spruce-clad doorway, which is like a giant framework around the room that lies beyond.

In this relaxed, albeit strikingly contemporary build, the living room's "dematerialized" rear walls allow seamless viewing—and indeed passage—to the deck and garden areas. To balance the huge window area, the full-height elevation behind the wood stove is dressed with mirror, which blurs the distinction between inside and out. The reflective glass is a masterstroke, actually, one that amplifies the sense of perceived depth in what is actually a modestly scaled room.

Stretching across the outdoor entertainment area, the barn's "shadow" is realized through a blackened timber pergola that doubly delivers: not only does it extend the building's line, it

1. The entertainment area is sheltered from sun and wind by a blackened wood "skeleton" pergola that's at once practical and beautiful.

2. The exterior boasts comfortable seating and dining zones, both of which satisfy the family's quest to spend as much time as possible alfresco.

1. The key to this external area's success is the fact that it's furnished, dressed and accessorized as if it were an internal room.

also acts as a screen to help buffer sun and wind. Accordingly, when it comes to architecture, the marriage of practicality and beauty wins every time, especially when paired from the initial stages of planning.

Sometimes, though, a little curveball can change the original concept, as it did here. Necessity being the mother of invention, the canopy evolved when the team realized that, to prevent long spans of roof timber warping, the gaps would have to be packed with stabilizing wooden blocks. But instead of spacing these in a regimented fashion, they were randomly scattered to filter light as if under a canopy of trees.

The interior design was driven by the architects, who custom-manufactured a number of furnishings and finishes, including the steel-fronted kitchen, wooden couches and the freestanding bathroom units and mirrors. At the same time, an inventory of jet-toned items was sourced, each piece chosen for its style and its ability to drive cohesion between zones.

We particularly like this house, which seems to have been envisioned to embrace (and perhaps improve) the passage of time. The kitchen counter material, for example, will age to echo nature. Fashioned from heat-treated blackened brass, the surface will mature, and, in doing so, will take on a gently oxidized patina.

We also admire the fact that nothing seems overplayed—particularly the roster of furniture, with most everything accorded asymmetrical positioning across the floor plan.

Playing angular forms against the occasional circular element helps temper the atmosphere, effectively ensuring that nothing in this darkly attired world feels austere or unwelcoming. Far from it, in fact: the clarity of space, simplicity of finish and unbalanced approach create a relaxed and casual elegance that draws visitors to the heart of the home.

The endgame? An escape just an hour from their city base, and the perfect backdrop against which the owners can embark upon the important business of the day—swimming, alfresco dinners and familial get-togethers where everyone can be, well, their very best selves.

We love surprises: the unassuming exterior, which blends seamlessly into the English countryside, provides little evidence of the modern architectural bounty that lies beyond.

Park Corner Barn

LOCATION
Chilterns, United Kingdom

COMPLETION YEAR
2011

OWNER
David McLaren

ARCHITECT
McLaren Excell

CONTRACTOR
BHL Builders

SIZE
4,575 sf (425 sqm)

NOTABLE BUILDING MATERIALS
Brick and flint with oak beams, limestone block fireplace, steel staircase

UTILITIES
On-grid supply

PHOTOGRAPHY
Hannah Taylor and McLaren Excell

For those who dream of escaping the hustle and bustle of life in London and immersing themselves in the tranquil English countryside, the lure of rural Oxfordshire (and its beauteous landscape) will most certainly appeal.

Just over an hour northwest of the nation's capital lies Chiltern Hills, the beautiful meadowlands that comprise this magnificent part of the world. Rich with cultural heritage and sporting some truly magnificent scenery, it's the perfect destination in which to create a dream retreat.

Set amongst beech-wooded farmland is one such dream, a beautiful structure known as Park Corner Barn. Built from traditional brick and flint in the late eighteenth century, and enlarged to twice its original size thanks to a Victorian addition in 1864, the barn was originally part of the neighbouring farm estate and was used as an agricultural threshing and cattle barn until the mid-nineties.

1. The exposed roof structure is at once practical and beautiful. Many of the barn's inherent features were smothered during its first residential conversion, as the previous owners sought to create a traditional house feel. This brave new version, however, embraces the past whilst framing it all in crisp white for the future.

2. A natural palette of sober materials evokes a sense of quiet tranquillity, therein allowing the fireplace (and overhead beams) to capture attention.

3. The rough timbers of the beams and the smooth finish of the doors create visual—and literal—texture. Mixing wood genera is something Mother Nature does in her forests, so follow her lead and *don't* feel compelled to match each piece of wood.

The current owner purchased the barn in 2009, some twelve years after it endured its first residential conversion, with the intention of stripping it back and starting over.

The first conversion of the barn in 1997, we learn, appears to have been an exercise in squeezing a maximum number of rooms into the building envelope, with low priority given to the rich materials and spatial qualities with which the structure overflows.

Swapping quantity for quality, the new plan serves fewer rooms with larger footprints, and places a greater emphasis on quality materials to create spaces that are light and atmospheric. The renovation involved significant restructuring—and replacement of many deteriorated timber elements—and, to facilitate this, the architectural team introduced a complicated package of concealed steelwork and structural timber framing.

As is the case with many heritage home renovations, the goal was to balance preservation with modernization whilst retooling the subject environment. And whilst tailoring this

particular (formerly agricultural) structure into a smart twenty-first-century escape, its visionaries pulled off a *major* triumph.

And so it came to pass that a space which once housed cattle now houses three bedrooms and two very large living areas. The opening up of the barn's south end created a vast double-height living room, rising up to the rafters of the main roof and into the gable ends on either side. Meanwhile, the previously isolated kitchen was knocked through to become part of the newly birthed open-concept space.

At the barn's north end, the removal of four boxy ensuite bedrooms provided space for a dedicated library and music room with proportions sufficient to accommodate thousands of books and records. For vinyl lovers like us, this room is absolute bliss: we can imagine stealing away with our favourite soundtrack, a good book and the ubiquitous glass of whisky. Yes indeed, we'd be gone for some time...

Inspired by the original structure, the south gable elevation is constructed from oversized sections of solid oak, with columns and beams imbuing the facade with an air of solidity and architectural rhythm. Echoing the barn's scale, the

1. Steel, stone and timber evoke their industrial past to become an inviting palette in this domestic environment.

2. Blond timber cabinets lend a Scandinavian edge and, coupled with concrete, the narrative is simple and strong.

3. The oak shelves provide order for an extensive book and music library: this is a great example of the way in which a "spare" room can be utilized to deliver uniquely appropriate function.

3

1. The enormous fireplace and chimney were conceived as one huge sculpted object: a composition of massive limestone blocks tapering to a lime-plastered flue echo the sloping forms of rural brick chimneystacks.

2. The geometry of the fire-place, hearth and shelf create undeniable interest in the living room. Consider how a few small details can collectively conspire a strong, confident statement.

3. We all live in box-like struc-tures, but it's what goes on inside that allows individuality to thrive. Here, a shelf and sliding door are competent partners in the elevation's overall aesthetic and function.

interior fit out is a case of "go big or go home," with an enormous fireplace and chimney conceived as one huge, sculptural object, a composition of massive limestone blocks that taper to a lime-plastered flue, to echo the sloping shapes of rural brick chimney stacks.

With such copious detailing to appreciate, it's hard *not* to be overwhelmed. Angles, everywhere, are precision-cut and plastered. Lines are true on every elevation. The oak doors, and joinery throughout, are masterfully executed and deliberately oversized, in keeping with the generous scale of their surroundings. It's clear—but in no way surprising—that every layer of the project has been thoughtfully planned.

What is surprising, however, is the staircase that links to the first floor: a moveable structure fabricated from steel, with a textured finish courtesy of the material's natural patina. The industrial feature serves its purpose as passage between floors,

1. Sliding barn doors are a welcome nod to the past, as well as being practical in terms of separating zones without consuming space. The large door size echoes the scale of the room to make a big, bold statement.

2. This is a perfect example of creating surprise when it's least expected. To make a retreat feel *really* special, consider its every inch and appraise what can be done to deliver arresting results at every turn.

3–6. To access the bedroom, the staircase is pushed to the centre of the room. When not required, it slides easily to the side to take up minimal space.

1. From artwork to walls, from flooring to textiles, quiet calm is born courtesy of a tactically muted colour palette.

2. The farmhouse sink is inspired by the barn's agricultural past: small details such as these can serve up big impact, even in a simple utility room.

but it's also a fascinating talking point: when bedroom access is required, the staircase can be pushed to the centre of the room to meet with the landing. When *not* required, it slides to the side to take up minimal space.

A second set of stairs leads to the master suite, where a bedroom, an open-plan bathroom with roll-top tub, and a well-appointed dressing area await to further cosset and reward.

That which most appeals (to us, certainly) is the uncomplicated vibe that abounds whilst navigating the space. Nothing feels overly complicated. White walls serve up a clean, gallery-like feel that permits roofing joists, structural beams and exposed brick areas to shine, in their own right, as important building components.

Across the entire landscape, a "less is more" attitude pervades—a restraint that, perhaps paradoxically, has been generously applied to materials, finishes and furnishings, each of which was selected for its contemporary simplicity. It's this concise palette of sober materials that ensures a sense of gathered consistency across the project: white-oiled oak, Bath limestone, Italian basalt and natural-fibre floor coverings amplify the overall sense of contemporary restraint. This reductive attitude towards tone and materiality allows the original fabric of the barn to withstand its additions and remain the predominant feature of the interior.

The big takeaway from this project? That (virtually) *any* property can be transformed into an ideal escape. Think of the visionaries who've transformed churches, shops and even grain silos into contemporary and very useable homes. And be inspired.

At Park Corner Barn, where once there was livestock, there's now the sweet lilt of music echoing out across an altogether gentle, pastoral life. A life that leaves the city *far* behind, to perfectly relax into the rural English countryside.

The recipe of stone, glass and Western red cedar sits well in this south-facing, multi-level home that follows the natural undulation of the landscape.

Plan B

LOCATION	**SIZE**
Haliburton, Ontario, Canada	3,250 sf (302 sqm) (including the bunkie)
COMPLETION YEAR	**NOTABLE BUILDING MATERIALS**
2015 (renovation)	Stick-built, pine-frame construction (main cabin), Western red cedar (post-and-beam sunroom and the bunkie), black-framed custom windows by euro + glasshaus; screened porch uses the Sunspace Sunrooms Weathermaster screen system; all structures set under raised-seam metal roofs
OWNERS	
Colin McAllister and Justin Ryan	
ARCHITECT	
Discovery Dream Homes	
INTERIOR DESIGNERS	**UTILITIES**
Colin McAllister and Justin Ryan	Electricity (on-grid supply), heating (electric with wood stove), water (well), waste (septic system)
CONTRACTORS	**PHOTOGRAPHY**
Randy Blain Construction (main cabin), Mason Brothers Construction (bunkie)	Robert Newnham

We looked at this formerly dilapidated cottage every day for perhaps two years before finally taking the plunge. Positioned literally next door to another from our own portfolio, we always thought it would benefit from a C+J revamp, but since our neighbours seemed happy in their home, we simply hadn't expected it to grace the market.

When their circumstances changed, however, they approached us to assess our interest in purchasing, to secure a sale without engaging a realtor. And who could blame them? With real estate commissions running around 4 percent, an off-market deal (with a realistic proposed selling price) is like gold dust, particularly from the seller's end of the bargain.

Whilst tackling another big project at the time *hadn't* been atop our radar, we were nonetheless interested, due—in part at

least—to the cabin's proximity to our own. A convenient project with just a one-minute commute? Aye, count us in.

So we had a little prod around, to appraise the opportunity, before returning next door to chat through the detail. Shortly thereafter, we made an offer: a bid, in actual fact, which was immediately agreeable to the sellers. And we took possession just six weeks later.

Our plan was simple: to transform the place into a private corporate retreat for large families and urbanites hell-bent on escaping the cut and thrust of city life. We knew there was a market in Haliburton for luxury rentals (our friend runs a holiday letting agency and frequently grumbles about inventory shortage) so, as a business model, it appeared to make sense. But there was massive work to be done. No, like *massive* work.

The rundown cottage, when we bought it, was certainly on the small side (our rental agency friends advised that to amplify its square footage would be to amplify its rental yield) so, as well as extending it with a sunroom to one side, we immediately looked at lifting it, in a similar manner to what we'd done next door, at Grey Gardens. The local planning department had looked favourably on that reno, so we reckoned we'd walk a relatively straightforward path with this one. Which in fact, we did, even though the weather conspired against us at almost every turn. Note to selves: never attempt another reno in the depths of a Canadian winter.

1. From humble beginnings, we coaxed this stretched-wood, jet-detailed ranch cabin with mid-century allusions. Indulgently dressed with a wrap-around Western red cedar deck, it boasts space sufficient to host large parties, both inside and out. Cladding the existing chimney with stone added a chunky visual layer that further enhances the rustic vibe.

2

2. In all the cabin projects we've built—or remodelled—we *always* add a screened porch or sunroom. Firstly and foremost, they're a great addition to cottage life (the extra space comes into its own on warmer days and nights); but secondly, any room that allows users to be "indoors," but with windows pulled open (courtesy of bug screens by Sunspace Sunrooms) and therefore immune to entomological attack, is a sure-fire winner. Generous interior layering (via textiles, accessories and lighting) conspires an invitation to relax.

To translate our vision, we hired Discovery Dream Homes to pen our project drawings and to submit plans to the township for approval. In association with our principal contractors Randy Blain Construction, they also erected the framework to accommodate our Sunspace Sunrooms Weathermaster screen system, as well as a separate log-built guest wing built, as a further subcontract, with Mason Brothers Construction, a Toronto-based company with whom we'd previously worked.

Discovery Dream Homes used 3D computer graphics, a state-of-the-art package that allowed us to "walk through" the proposed changes before work had even begun. The virtual modelling skills blew us away; the company's assistance with structural issues was second to none; and, as an invaluable design conduit between Randy and all other team players, they delivered a masterful vision.

The re-versioned cabin has four bedrooms, three bathrooms, a games room, two living rooms, a chef's kitchen, an outdoor dining room, two sunrooms, a fully fitted laundry room (complete with washer and dryer) and a large covered carport.

We designed an interior to meet the potential holiday rental sector head-on. Against a backdrop of predominantly white

paint, we layered in as much comfort as we could to indulge guests at every turn. And wood: lots of it. Every ceiling is dressed with "fine line" milled Western red cedar. We always have an eye trained on the environment, and since Western red cedar is so responsibly forested, it's eminently more sustainable than other lumber types. Plus it's easy to work with and, as we see it, actually improves with age.

The master bedroom suite measures twenty-five by eleven feet and incorporates a large king bed, nightstands, a wardrobe and a seating area. At one end, custom barn doors roll open and closed, behind them a fully tricked-out bathroom with a hefty stone sink sits on a leggy base. With windows on either side (one a fixed panel, and the other an operable "door" in the shower enclosure so guests can embrace the great outdoors whilst showering), it's a bright space that proved a massive hit with renters.

Next to this principal suite are two smaller—yet amply proportioned—bedrooms and a cement-tiled bathroom, whilst down

1. A wood bed and nightstands set a chunky tone, but we softened proceedings with white, pin-tuck cotton bedding and yellow detailing. An assembly of mirrors (the grouping is redolent of fish scales) makes a big statement above the bed.

2. With windows on either side of a trough sink, the ensuite wash zone is a bright and welcoming space. We laid the ceramic wood-look flooring in the same direction as the real wood flooring in the bedroom. This continuous finish is a small detail, but it helps to visually combine both zones.

3. Western red cedar cladding and a modern log burning stove serve up a welcoming corner where guests can pull up a chair and enjoy whisky and card games.

the corridor is the kitchen diner which overlooks a sunken living room whose configuration is a reminder of the 1980s, when our cabin was originally built.

The moniker "Ikea kitchen in drag" stuck from the moment it was uttered by one of our team whilst touring the completed food-prep and dining zone at Plan B. It's fair to say that our rustic reversion is perfect proof (were it ever required) that you don't have to spend a fortune to have a stylish abode. It depends, quite simply, upon where you shop. Consider indeed the big blue and yellow, a retailer of which we're big fans. The Swedish store's kitchen aisles have long since been our default when budgets are limited. Whether "suburban modern," "cutting edge" or "rustic cottage," it all comes down to what you do with what you've got.

In our favour was ample square footage. As such, we positioned a large quartz island, "wrapped" to the floor at either end. Installing unbroken counter is relatively straightforward (for an expert), but to master invisible-bond ninety-degree corners, professional fabrication and installation are required.

We worked with House of Granite, whose corners—as well as their cuts for the Blanco sink and hob—are perfection itself. Set within the island is a whisper-quiet dishwasher (noise bleed in the open-plan area is negligible) as well as countless drawers which more than accommodate everything required for cottage life.

We extended the kitchen island's width to facilitate breakfasting, but rather than leave the underside plain, we installed barnboard to complement the flooring that runs underfoot. Overhead hang two spun-metal shades, dramatic pendants that more than brighten the counter when daylight fades.

Continuing our jet-detailed vision, the prevailing look is at once crisp and modern. Being that lumber finishes are such an important part of the overall aesthetic, we embellished the windows with wood Venetians accented with black tapes to provide light screening, as required. It's a great-quality, but nonetheless basic-buy, flat-pack kitchen in pristine white, thoroughly re-identified with all the extra elements such as quartz, barnboard and great lighting. Post transformation, it boasts heaps of character, but it was far from a "drag" to create.

To visually embolden the living room and infuse a warm, welcoming edge, we positioned a box-shaped stove, set on an asymmetrical poured concrete base, as a wonderful focal point in a predominantly white-painted scheme. Thick-weave wicker

1. Anchored around a large Ikea table sit café chairs and a beautiful bench, manufactured (using reclaimed factory floorboards and beams) by Mark Livingston of Rebarn. The mellow wood tones help conjure the relaxed cottage vibe we so keenly sought to create.

2. The wall behind? Well, dressing an unusually shaped area such as this can be tricky. To problem-solve, we arranged a collection of artworks (this works better than one large piece), the quirky pieces a fun nod to collections of old, and a great conversation starter when guests arrive.

3. Wood flooring, wicker sofas and leather club chairs distill a relaxed vibe, dressed in front of the Stûv fireplace asymetrically positioned on a concrete base.

sofas dressed with orange, black and natural-toned toss pillows provide the room with texture, as does a woven-top Indonesian bench which we specified as a coffee table.

Outdoors, the action continues. Plan B's external vernacular is contemporary, with board-and-batten Cape Cod Grey–painted cedar siding. Arranged under a black steel roof—parts of which overhang the deck to provide year-round shelter—it's a commanding structure, yet one that seems to disappear into the forest as viewed from the lake.

There's a carport, a two-bedroom, log-built bunkie, a near 2,000-sf (186-sqm) deck and an outdoor spa comprising hot tub, shower and five-person sauna. The area more than delivers market expectation as far as renters are concerned. We've built many decks and patios in our time, and our go-to lumber is always (just like it is indoors) Western red cedar.

Importantly, as the deck ages and the wood genus matures, it "silvers" to a beautiful soft sheen. That's why, more times than we care to remember, we've forgone varnish or stain, opting instead to let Mother Nature deliver the warmly metallic grey-scale lustre she so beautifully composes.

1–4. The guest annex, constructed as it is from square-cut cedar logs, provides two full bedrooms, a three-piece bathroom, and a living room, all wrapped into an approximately 500-sf (46-sqm) footprint. Sure, the individual spaces aren't enormous, but their proportions are sufficient enough to makes guests feel indulged.

BE GREAT OUTDOORS

Follow our guide to make more of your alfresco experience during warmer months.

Your deck is your living room, dining room and party zone, so ensure it's functional *and* beautiful.

GIVE YOUR OUTDOOR SPACE AN IDENTITY

It's simply not enough to have a bare deck or patio. Instead, use the space to cure a short-fall you may have indoors. Maybe your house doesn't have room for entertaining? Then install a table and chairs outside to create a seasonal dining space that can be enjoyed when the weather is fine.

ADD SERVICES TO MAKE LIFE EASIER

It's *so* worth installing outdoor electrical, gas and water supplies to service your deck, patio or yard. Having gas for cooking, electricity for music and lighting, as well as running water to keep your patio clean and your plants well-watered makes so much sense.

CREATE AN OUTDOOR KITCHEN

From chefs poised at sophisticated built-in cooking stations to dads sizzling at the barbecue, the summer belongs to fresh-air food prep. These days even the most basic big-box stores offer a stellar selection of grills and barbeques, so head on in and prepare to fire up your inner chef.

DON'T LET THE BUGS BUG

Nobody wants to be eaten alive by mosquitoes, but similarly, nobody—particularly as the warmer weather takes hold—dreams of being shut away indoors to avoid the terror of entomological attack. Avoid pools of standing water in overflowing planters, which attracts mosquitoes. Use citronella candles, or plant marigolds or lavender to keep bugs naturally at bay.

USE SUN POWER

Solar power and low-wattage lighting have grown in terms of technology, efficiency and afford-ability, so invest in some sun-powered illumination to make your outdoor area sparkle. From path stakes to silk-shaded pendants, there are solar-powered options for all occasions.

KEEP COOL

Fend off the sun with auspicious planting, or by using a patio umbrella or awning. An outdoor fan would make a great ally to help moderate temperatures, as would an exterior misting system: examples of both are readily available in big-box stores. Why sweat and sizzle when you can slumber in the shade?

WARM IT UP

When the nights start to cool, you'll soon find yourself looking for ways to stay outdoors a little longer. An outdoor fireplace, fire pit or patio heater could be the answer. We have a Solus Decor gas-powered fire bowl at our cottage and even use it in the depths of winter for a flaming good time in the snow…

PLANTING

Soften up your deck or patio with a little auspicious planting. Hanging baskets bursting with colour look amazing, whilst tall trees in smart planters ooze sophistication. And worry not if you don't have green fingers: don't say no … say *faux*. It's time to fake it with realistic topiary set into modern tubs and troughs.

LET YOUR FURNITURE TELL A DESIGN STORY

From traditional rattan to modern white and steel, there are many variants of outdoor furniture to spell out a strong design story on your patio. Maybe the Raffles Hotel look is your go-to alfresco style? Or perhaps it's Miami chic or the Adirondack vibe? Whatever you choose, start planning those outdoor moments *now*. Bear in mind that most good garden and deck furniture will disappear from stores before summer has even started.

ACCESSORIZE, ACCESSORIZE, ACCESSORIZE

If you can't stretch to a whole new look for your patio, dock or deck, create an updated look for less with accessories. Be bold with cushions, outdoor throws and pillows. Add candle storm lamps, pitchers, glasses and outdoor accessories to bring joy to a lifeless space. But keep it simple. Less, as is so often the case, is more.

MAKE MEAL TIMES A GROUP EFFORT

Make it easy on yourself by utilizing the skills of your guests and sharing the workload. If one of your friends, for example, is a master barbecuer, assign them grilled-dish duty so you can get on with what you're good at. Cocktails, anybody?

CREATE A SUMMERTIME PLAYLIST

Pre-set music on your phone or digital streaming service to set the mood and provide a soundtrack for the day. You are the best DJ, after all…

Whilst the cabin's exterior was designed to mimic local barn buildings, closer inspection reveals glimpses of the structure's residential nature.

Reeds Bay

LOCATION
Reeds Bay, Ontario,
Canada

COMPLETION YEAR
2010

OWNERS
Peter Schneider and
Richard Almonte (and their
beautiful West Highland
Terrier, Lucy)

ARCHITECT
superkül

CONTRACTOR
Truehaven Design Build

SIZE
1,300 sf (121 sqm)

NOTABLE BUILDING MATERIALS
Wood construction, Hardie board
and cedar exterior cladding set
under a steel roof

UTILITIES
Electricity (on-grid supply), heating
(wood stove), water (shore well),
waste (septic system)

PHOTOGRAPHY
Shai Gil

Constructed upon the largest island in the Thousand Islands archipelago, this simple two-bedroom respite, owned by Torontonians Peter Schneider and Richard Almonte, takes design cues from traditional long barns, with angular sections incised from the main structure to afford weather-protected exterior "porches" and expansive views of beautiful Lake Ontario.

Envisioned by its owners in conjunction with their architects, the underplayed exterior is clad in a siding that looks like a regular wood product, but is in actual fact a weather-proof concrete product painted grey. The entire building sits under a slick steel roof that dutifully protects the structure from the elements.

Upon approach, the cabin could easily be misinterpreted as some type of storage facility, devoid, as it is, of windows as viewed from the road, with only a door (accessed via a walkway flanked with thick grasses) to punctuate the minimalistic veneer.

1. A wooden boardwalk cleaves its way towards the entrance across a grassy plain, flanked on either side by tall grasses that create a sheltered walkway. It's a simple demarcation, but it makes a stout, graphic statement.

2. The house features an attached storage "shed" recessed to the side of the outdoor seating area (note no handles or visible hinges to clutter the vision), tall enough to take canoes and ladders. superkül designed this feature, as per their clients' request, to include a covered seating area in front. Visual contrast is played out as the porch area's warm wood finish meets the cool-toned exterior cladding.

Step across the threshold, and the uncomplicated aesthetic continues. Unfussy, though certainly not spartan, and dressed with a carefully curated inventory of *objets trouvés,* new finds and inherited antiques, the mood is modestly underplayed.

It's a somewhat tricky science, though, to discern scale or number of rooms here—because internal doors aren't visible until passage is made through the living area and down the long hallway. There, a master bedroom and ensuite bathroom are located, and a hidden stairway leads to a guest bedroom and a neatly arranged home office.

It's rather lovely, actually, to visit an interior whose atmosphere feels every bit as fresh as it looks. That's the holy grail (as we see it, certainly) of a well-composed project: balancing visuals and heart in equal measure.

And balance is what it's all about. "We're fortunate to spend as many as three nights a week here between May and October," explains Schneider.

His partner Almonte picks up the point: "We're both busy with work, so having this cabin affords us the luxury of much-needed weekly decompression. And that enhancement to life just can't be quantified."

As a backdrop to the expertly curated interior, walls are ship-lap clad and painted in an unassuming bone tone. At one end of the kitchen/dining/living space, a simple log-burning stove sends a massive chimney snaking upwards to release its smoky charge.

Almonte and Schneider explain that the stove isn't just pretty to watch as the flames dance within the appliance: it's also, by their account, highly serviceable and provides sufficient heat to warm the house.

Wandering, there's a fresh feel at every turn, with passive ventilation courtesy of operable windows and skylights. The airy cottage is organized by a narrow double-height corridor that navigates the rear of the building, with living and sleeping quarters arranged to face the lake.

1. We admire log fires in any application, but in the cottage space they seem most at home. This appliance has a modern line that doesn't complicate the wall in front of which it sits, and whilst its tall snaking exhaust pipe is obviously a required vent, it's also a sculptural addition in this simple room.

2–3. The kitchen—underplayed, to the max. Basic white cabinetry ensures the zone remains visually uncluttered. There's ample space to satisfy food prep requirements and storage, even though the cabin's owners elected not to hang eye-level cabinets so as to maximize the elevation's depth. A marble island serves up dependability, its solid lines playing in beautiful contrast to the painted wood finishes that surround the kitchen.

When square footage is compromised, an effective way to maximize the feeling of space is with architectural verticality, a practice that's clearly visible in this project. Sightlines are elevated via the tall ceilings, and further enhanced courtesy of ten-foot windows that flood the area with natural light, whilst providing perfect lake and garden vistas. Upstairs, the loft contains a second bedroom as well as a simply appointed home office, the zones afforded unique spatial dynamics thanks to the steeply pitched roof.

Oh yes, that roof. Its deeply angled nature delivers, internally, a marriage of converging angles and lines that distract from the fact the cottage is actually somewhat compact. The structure's limited square footage, though, doesn't get in the way of its livability. Not even remotely.

Filming one of our TV shows, we spent the day with Almonte and Schneider and discovered they live life large in their

1. White painted shiplap creates a clean, gallery like feel: the perfect backdrop to showcase classic mid-mod furniture.

2. Learn to see things differently: an upturned travel trunk is reimagined as a convenient nightstand.

3. A corridor of tall grasses delineates the dramatic runway that leads into this Reeds Bay retreat.

beautiful home from home. With a busy existence in Toronto, their respite provides, says Almonte, "a sense of calm, and all the peace we need, when most we need it." Schneider adds: "Decompression settles from the moment we escape the city to come here. Honestly, the minute we jump in our car we can feel it."

It may not be enormous, but it's a frequent gathering point for friends and family who enjoy the cabin's relaxed atmosphere, and it says so much about their hosts. Each artifact proudly displayed was collected over time, each piece of furniture either inherited, salvaged or bought during the couple's travels.

Yes indeed, the interior fit out references the couple's attitude to entertaining: a relaxed informality is present, with several commentators observing there's an almost church-like feel to the cabin's pared-back style. Holy or otherwise, the congregation who visit are assured of a soothing environment in which prayers for relaxation are almost certain to be answered.

A beacon of light in the darkness: when the cabin is occupied, lanterns make it glow like a firefly in the forest as people approach. The simple shape of the structure makes it immediately recognizable as a place of shelter.

Refuge Free Lab

LOCATION
Bay of Fundy, Nova
Scotia, Canada

COMPLETION YEAR
2014

OWNERS
Talbot Sweetapple and
Diana Carl

ARCHITECT
MacKay-Lyons
Sweetapple Architects

CONTRACTOR
Dalhousie School of
Architecture Free Lab
students

SIZE
500 sf (46 sqm)

NOTABLE BUILDING MATERIALS
Hemlock wood beams and floor
joists, spruce stud framing and interior
finishes, white cedar shingle wrap
roof and long exterior walls, hemlock-
cladded gable ends

UTILITIES
Electricity (none, battery-
operated lanterns are used),
heating (wood stove), waste
(outhouse composting toilet)

PHOTOGRAPHY
William Green Photography

For us, the notion of experiencing a rural retreat is all about bringing people together, connecting with nature and sharing optimal decompression in the great outdoors.

Whilst conceptualizing Refuge, a multi-purpose shelter overlooking the Bay of Fundy in Nova Scotia, architects MacKay-Lyons Sweetapple advanced this notion by using the project's design and construction to inform and educate students at the Dalhousie University School of Architecture. The cabin's realization took the idea of "sharing the experience" to an entirely new level: from the ground up.

Developed as part of a design and build program at Dalhousie, the beautiful refuge was constructed by architecture students, who were guided throughout the *entire* process by teachers and local craftspeople. This annually held program provides students with hands-on building experience (to complement

1–2. Salvation at the end of the journey—the perforated screen design creates a lantern effect by night.

studio-based learning), the objective being to develop an understanding of wood in the history of construction, particularly lumber-building practices pertaining to the Minas Basin region of Nova Scotia.

It's a wonderful example, as we see it, of a project where local practices have been shared, group sensibilities enjoyed, and the next generation of visionaries informed and enthused.

But skill-setting aside, it all comes down to creating an abode that can be enjoyed in the present-day context, and indeed far into the future. The principal difference with this place, however, is that it was built for public use, as opposed to privately constructed for personal use and the enjoyment of family and friends.

But the goal is the same: to fashion an environment that's all about rest and recuperation from the stresses of modern life. Any well-conceived cabin should have a soul-feeding alchemy; it should be a magical experience. The position of this simple, gabled structure (in a protected clearing, sheltered by a proud oak tree) not only amplifies the idea of being protected, but it adds spirit to the mix... to the power of ten.

This spiritual quality exists, perhaps, because the tiny structure is positioned to allow the sun, the large central table, the

windows, the bay and the cape to be in perfect axial alignment during the summer solstice sunset. But of course none of this was an accident: it was expertly planned by Talbot Sweetapple and his team.

As viewed from its front elevation, the structure appears to float above the forest, held aloft by sonotubes, with entry across a large wooden deck and through an inset porch. The central gathering space is flanked by a series of sleeping nooks and anchored by various totemic elements (namely the central table, counter and hearth), which provide utility, focus and warmth.

Facing the entry, a second inset porch opens to a large floating deck (aligned to the northwest)—perfect for enjoying views of the nearby maritime landscape, a combination of wetlands, pastures, forests and the beautiful shoreline.

The project focused on innovative use of locally sourced wood—down to the very timbers that serve as the structural system of walls, floors and roof. The building's exposed elements (beams and floor joists) were lovingly built using hemlock—chosen for its rot-resisting prowess—while the protected structure (stud framing) and interior finishes are all spruce.

Every detail was exactingly planned to ensure the cabin remained impervious to the elements and (as much as possible)

1. Guests tend to think of the Refuge as a spiritual, almost church-like respite. In its own right, it's a monument to the Bay of Fundy.

2. The overhead loft serves as an ideal storage area—zones such as this are essential in a small space, especially when decompression is on the agenda. Clutter, of course, is the enemy of relaxation.

3. The building is situated to take advantage of light as it pours into the cabin. Visiting, there's an amazing sense of warmth and stillness.

2

3

1. Light floods through the hemlock screens, casting shadows and decorating the walls with pattern. Keeping to basics, the cabin offers uncomplicated succour: a place to rest and eat. There's no electricity, running water or septic system, but there's a separate outhouse for guest convenience.

2. The filtered view to the bay offers privacy and shelter from the sun as the doors swing to capture fresh breezes on warm summer days.

3. A wood-burning stove generates enough heat to warm the cabin, even on the most frigid Canadian days. Imagine sitting by the fire on a cold winter's morning as the snow falls gently outside. Imagine that sense of comfort and well-being. And *breathe*...

the passage of time. The roof and long exterior walls, for example, are wrapped with white cedar shingles, which contain natural preservatives and are therefore well adapted to the local climate.

The cabin's gable ends are clad with vertical hemlock screening that serves as a rain barrier, whilst delivering a dramatic lighting effect inside that's reminiscent of agricultural barns. At night this effect is reversed as the building becomes a glowing lantern in the woods. It's simple, yet at once breathtakingly atmospheric.

The Refuge's function is geared towards sheltering those in the locale. Situated on a densely forested headland overlooking the Bay of Fundy, it's a resting place, on an existing trail, for local community groups; a warming hut for skiers; a gathering spot for the local horse-riding club, and a reprieve from the elements, as and when required, for fishermen.

This, as we see it, is what makes this cabin such a heartfelt community asset. The keyword, quite clearly, is *sharing*. "On special occasions," explains Sweetapple, "we'll gather to cook local game harvested on the property. With notice, the local bass fisherman will leave a fish, and the waterfowl hunters will generously donate some of their harvest. Pheasant stew, smoked black duck and baked bass are just some of the dishes we, or those that use the cabin, like to cook."

The Refuge Free Lab certainly packs considerable punch as a valuable community resource, as a learning tool in wood-building and as the perfect place to escape to, break bread (with friends or strangers) and watch the seasons change over the bay. Okay, so it might be tiny, but the welcome it proffers is Jurassic. It's a magical retreat, one that warms the hearts and nurtures the spirit of those who come when most they need escape.

This red-roofed log cabin could be the poster child for anyone who dreams of escaping the city, igniting their frontier spirit and connecting with nature.

THE LUXURY LOG HOME

Sucker
Lake Cabin

LOCATION
Sucker Lake, Ontario,
Canada

COMPLETION YEAR
2014

OWNERS
Colin McAllister and Justin
Ryan with two co-investors

INTERIOR DESIGNERS
Colin McAllister and
Justin Ryan

CONTRACTORS
Dan McNeill of Metal Edge
Construction (main cabin),
Bateman Fine Cabinetry
(kitchen)

SIZE
1,500 sf (139 sqm)

NOTABLE BUILDING MATERIALS
Principal level constructed from
round-cut pine logs with stick-
frame construction on the lower
and attic levels, structure set
under a steel roof

UTILITIES
Electricity (on-grid supply),
heating (electric with log-
burning fire), water (well), waste
(independent septic system)

PHOTOGRAPHY
Brandon Barré

Fact: there's something quintessentially North American about a red-roofed, log-built cabin. It's a classic vacation-home style that screams Canadian, and it's an aesthetic that's ambitiously chased by many of our own clients.

Perched, as this one is, on the edge of a hill, beside a small, private lake in Muskoka (one of Canada's pre-eminent vacation districts), it's a cute-as-you-like holiday respite, and one in which we saw so much potential when we first spied it some years ago on a cold, dark December day.

From the moment we breezed into the main open-plan living-kitchen-dining area, we knew we could reinvigorate the cottage, which, as we found it, had been lost to the ravages of time with an interior fit out that owed more to the 1980s than it did the

2

1. On this console, two large glass-drummed lamps (the empty bases of which we filled with thick rope found in a boating supplies store) set a balanced note, whilst jet-toned mirrors amplify the twin-sided arrangement.

2. Hand-built and painted grey, this kitchen was a veritable joy to create. We outsized the quartz island to provide ancillary dining function and illuminated the scene with nickel-plated storm lamp pendants. The fridge and freezer are concealed behind tall doors.

cooler end of vacation home-style. But we've always loved a challenge...

We tore away damaged floorboards, an old pine kitchen, and two wildly outdated bathrooms. We punched through a solid wood wall to insert glass doors, through which to enjoy the lake vistas. (In the cottage's previous incarnation, somewhat bizarrely, there were only tiny windows on the front elevation.) And with the interior stripped clean of everything that had previously shackled it to the past, we set about effecting change to pull it, kicking and screaming, into the modern day.

We elected to create an interior schematic that would provide exactly what the market—whenever we decided to either sell or rent it—would expect. The Muskoka lakes, you see, have long been considered one of Canada's most desirable vacation pockets (it's often compared to the Hamptons), so the aesthetic we elected to elicit was an upmarket lodge vibe with thick, luxuriant layers and generous use of linens and leather. Mood is relaxed, with low lighting, faux horn detailing and comfortable upholstery at every turn.

Our realtors, mindful we'd eventually be exposing the house to the market (in some shape or form), agreed with our sentiment that the cabin should be indulged with the feel of a mountain lodge or ski chalet. It simply made sense to cater to the area's demographic, and it's a classic aesthetic that's proved popular with buyers and renters alike. That said, we elected to take our cabin project to the next level.

Log homes, we've discovered, if poorly lit, can be a little on the dark side. To remedy this, we modified lighting and highlighted construction features—such as the points at which logs cross and ceiling beams intersect—to frame the building's structure. We're not talking massive changes, just a few simple adjustments (a pin spot here or a light pool there) to provide dramatic, visual return.

The top and basement floors (initially drywalled and therefore less significant than the main floor) were eventually clad,

1. In this log cabin, the systematic layering creates atmosphere, making everything feel relaxed, friendly and decidedly welcoming. For example, the specification of soft linen upholstery paired with a French button-tufted leather ottoman delivers a generous measure of comfort that further softens the environment.

2. In a home constructed primarily from solid lumber, edges can, without due care and attention, appear hard or indeed unwelcoming. But not on our watch. Not ever. As designers, our projects should always feel indulgent and welcoming at every turn. Typically, we bring the pursuit of comfort back to one simple word: atmosphere.

1. To soften the harder-edged pine-strapped walls, we designed and specified an outsized padded headboard. Shots of plaid via drapery and a touchy-feely armoury of cushions and throws provide visual and literal comfort. We pushed this colour scheme through rolling barn doors and into the connecting lounge area.

2. We call this style "bleak chic." Inspired by a fall-out-shelter sign we spotted in New York City, we combined dark grouted subway tile with medium-toned grey ceramic tile. A cast concrete sink adds a utilitarian feel, whilst bulk-head lights ($20 a pop from big box stores) suffuse the project with an industrial edge.

in places, with rough sawn lumber board to continue the woody appeal of the cabin's principal floor. A brand-new handcrafted and hand-painted kitchen was added, whilst new bathrooms were installed to infuse the project with contemporary flair.

Focused on creating high-end "rustic luxe," we specified a careful mix of antique pieces and contemporary store-bought items, with the emphasis placed firmly on rustic. Whilst Muskoka isn't a skiing destination per se, it's an area with particularly bleak winters and seismic snowfall. Chasing a warm, indulgent lodge vibe more than made sense.

We remain super proud of this project, and hope you're inspired by its various layers. The realization of its schematic directive (issued by our toughest clients: ourselves) was relatively straightforward. With "atmosphere" our perpetual watchword, we simply opened the space and let the light flood in. And we layered, and then layered some more.

1. Good background and foreground are the holy grail of any decorator. When colouration is correctly assembled, that is when the magic truly happens. To bring any scheme alive (not least one in a woody environment such as this), it's imperative you add extra dimension to build the textures of light and shade.

2. Creating mirrored balance suffuses the proceedings with a sense of order. In the urban setting where interiors are typically pared back, forced symmetry can feel austere. At the cottage, where enhanced decorative layers are often present, the pursuit of symmetry produces a sense of well-being.

Light, fantastic—punching an aperture to accommodate three sets of French doors was our first port of transformative call. Be mindful, however, as you appraise a project such as this, that structural integrity can be easily undermined if you don't pay proper attention to sequence. It's an abiding C+J maxim: to fail to plan is to plan to fail. If you rush in without first assessing structural load, you'll (potentially) run into huge issues.

Fortunately, we didn't need to install a header beam: the log walls, auspiciously cut as we created the apertures for the doors, retained sufficient integrity. However, take a tip: a licensed contractor will guide you through this potential minefield. If you're not working with a contractor, and if you have even the vaguest concern, it's imperative you seek structural guidance. The last thing you need is for a load-bearing wall to collapse into space once occupied by a window or a door.

TEN WAYS TO BRING THE FEEL-GOOD FACTOR INTO YOUR HOME

Second homes and vacation properties tend to be bought from the heart (more than the head) with owners looking for an experience that's both re-balancing and life-changing. Ensure yours delivers what you need by nurturing the "feel-good factor" at every turn, to bring out the best in you and your guests. Small changes, planned carefully, can add up to huge reward. And remember that it's as much about spending time to get it right as it is spending money.

The best escapes are birthed when you follow your heart: forget fashions and trends if you *truly* want to suffuse your cabin with the happiness factor.

CHANGE UP YOUR FABRICS

Lighten up rooms by swapping heavy fabrics for lighter alternatives. In the living room, remove thick curtains and replace with a crisp white blind and diaphanous sheers. Change wintery knitted sofa cushions and throws for linen and cotton alternatives, and pepper a plain scheme with occasional shots of colour to add a dash of summer. In the bedroom, employ crisp cotton bedding and add soft cashmere throws for a touch of luxury.

GO BACK TO THE LAND

Create a veritable market garden at home by using fruits and vegetables as colourful room accessories. Pop a dozen lemons into a clear glass orb vase for a modern burst of colour in the kitchen, dress your dining table with a basket of fresh carrots, onions and lettuce or use ornamental cabbages as floral arrangements on a table centrepiece.

BE CASUAL WITH FLOWERS

Try ditching formal floral arrangements in favour of lazy, casual flower bunches. Be inspired by your garden and place foliage and flowers in a much more organic way—use lots of small, delicate blooms and mix with droopy foliage. Ditch the crystal vases and instead use large milk jugs, teapots and tins for a farmhouse feel.

HARMONIOUS HOME = HARMONIOUS MIND

Arrange your cabin into distinct zones to keep the design clean and fresh, and be sure to utilize every inch of space. Keep things you need stored out of sight but close at hand to create an efficient environment.

BRING THE OUTDOORS IN

Keep main windows clear so guests can walk up to the glass and enjoy the vista beyond. When it comes to furniture, indoor wicker immediately makes us think of the great outdoors and of exotic terraces basking in extreme temperatures. And don't think you have to spend loads of money: instead, shop smart in second-hand stores, garage sales and flea markets. You'll be amazed at what you'll find. Antique garden tools, sun-baked benches and weather-beaten painted signs will bring outdoor escapism inside *without* breaking the bank.

ADD TEXTURAL ELEMENTS

Add texture to add comfort: layers work just as well in summer as they do in winter, so add various textiles to amplify the touchy-feely element. Specify rolled-up bamboo blinds and swap heavy floor rugs for natural alternatives such as seagrass and sisal to proffer a cool, beachy vibe.

A CLEAN HOUSE IS A HAPPY HOUSE

Nothing feels fresher than a wonderfully clean environment, so find time to take spring cleaning to the next level. Clean, uncluttered rooms always feel larger and fresher, so weed out items you no longer love, use or need and provide storage for the items you want to hold on to. And the best way to encourage that uplifting summer light to flood in? Ensure windows are sparklingly crystal-clear, to brighten your home … for free.

CHANGE YOUR DIET

If the contents of your fridge consist of bars of lard, whole milk and box upon box of ready-made meals, perhaps it's time to lighten up in more ways than one. A change of diet this season will make you feel so much better and, when teamed with a greater regime of physical activity, you'll soon see weight loss and attitude improvement, not to mention a betterment to your skin, which will take on a whole new summer glow.

The five ways to fitness are:
1. Set realistic goals
2. Stick to a schedule
3. Stay busy
4. Get physical
5. Think carefully about what you eat!

DON'T BE COLD, BE BOLD!

Mother Nature is undoubtedly at her boldest during summer months with her bursts of vivid colour and large, bright flowers, so follow suit and be inspired by her dramatic gusto. Swap plain crockery for floral motifs and hang bold botanical artwork to bring the garden inside.

ADD COLOUR

The simplest way to create a fresh summer feel is to replace darkness with light—and that means reaching for the paintbrush. Be inspired by flowers, greenery and the summer sun and use a tonal palette that feels warmly seasonal. Stay on trend by moving away from neutral shades (like cream and bone) and instead express yourself with naturals like bark, moss and stone. Blue and white will immediately make you feel like you're at the beach, whilst painted horizontal stripes will evoke clapboard New England homesteads.

Island life—this residence comprises
a quartet of interconnected volumes
that join at a central open courtyard.

Tiny Holiday Home

LOCATION
Vinkaveen, Netherlands

COMPLETION YEAR
2019

OWNERS
Mira Huussen and
Sjef Peeraer

ARCHITECTS
Chris Collaris Architects
and i29 interior architects

INTERIOR DESIGNERS
Chris Collaris Architects
and i29 interior architects

CONTRACTOR
Hagoort Bouw

SIZE
590 sf (55 sqm)

NOTABLE BUILDING MATERIALS
Wood skeleton set on a concrete
foundation, polished concrete
floors, waxed wood-facade cladding,
oak interior finishes

UTILITIES
On-grid supply with radiant
in-floor heating

PHOTOGRAPHY
Ewout Huibers

Imagine a cube, exploding from its epicentre to form four component parts. Then visualize those components as the basis of a modern home from home. That's precisely what the owners of this respite did, in conjunction with their architects, when conceptualizing the small—but perfectly formed—retreat.

As an arrangement of blocky angles and expertly planned perpendiculars, it's a clever configuration that maximizes the usability of its every square inch.

Many of today's rural abodes set out to blur the lines between outdoors and in, with large windows or exterior decks designed to optimize the fresh-air existence of their users. And it's a remit, of course, that makes perfect sense: especially where smaller spaces are concerned. Who wouldn't want to spill over, climate

permitting, into the clutch of Mother Nature's more generous square footage?

In this summer home in Vinkeveense Plassen, a marshy area of lakes and peninsulas in the Netherlands, the connection to the great outdoors is forged by positioning rooms around what's essentially a courtyard: one that becomes the heart of the home when doors are pushed back to create the ultimate indoor/outdoor terrain.

And what makes this one special? Well, it's just so darned uncomplicated and pure. Nothing is overplayed and the space is beautifully articulated—both visually and ergonomically—as transition is made from zone to zone.

Yes indeed, it's a dutifully low-key affair, one that's carved into a beautiful location surrounded by clear water and abundant natural greenery to protect the site from wind. But all the time it's just an eleven-mile bike ride from bustling Amsterdam. Aye, for the social quotient who like their seclusion with a side order of city fun, this wee place ticks *all* the boxes.

Designed by i29 interior architects in collaboration with Chris Collaris Architects, the cabin replaced an older property that occupied the same spot. "We endeavoured to keep it simple,"

1. The cubist shapes join with nature to wall up the garden and add to the sense of privacy and escapism.

2. In the outdoor shower, a powder-coated steel ladder provides a sculptural element and useful storage for towels. Matching finishes and colours create continuity and a benign sense of completion.

3. Keeping trims and surrounds hidden, and using the same finish on doors and walls, simplifies the architecture and poses a "Where is the door?" conundrum that's only answered by the walkway's position.

4. A combination of painted and natural finishes generally works well. Here, the black-waxed timber exterior recedes into the background, providing definition to the lush natural greenery.

explains Collaris. "Not least because everything had to come by boat, with a minimal number of journeys to help tailor overall project costs. Accordingly, most of the building happened on site, with everything assembled by a team of skilled carpenters."

With strict height and size stipulations restricting the footprint to a modest 600 sf (56 sqm), the team worked hard to realize a small home which wouldn't only work well, but which would look interesting as viewed across its every exterior elevation.

Remarkably, for all its modest scale, there's a generous feeling of space, with abundant natural light and panoramic views—once again, from every elevation—to the surrounding topography. The project is divided into four blocky pavilions,

each set around a courtyard. From outside, each offers diversity in size and function, but when interconnected they create a complete sculptural template that lends itself perfectly to modern life.

In order to intensify the building's sculptural strength, all facades are clad in black-waxed timber with invisible roof-endings detailed *behind* the wood facade, to further pursue the minimal aesthetic. This seamlessness continues across the large windows, and indeed the sliding doors, merging indoors with out. At the same time, a continuous concrete floor joins all areas at its epicentre to further blur boundaries.

One of the cabin's most striking, yet simple, achievements is witnessed via its restrained use of colour. A palette of black and pale oak appears throughout, sandwiched, at all times, between white ceilings and a polished concrete floor. At every turn, the

1. When half the home is outdoors, a monochrome colour palette is all that's required. All other colour comes from changing light of day, changes in the weather and the change of season. It's a space that redecorates itself on a perfect loop.

2. Using the same concrete floor, both indoors and out, provides a platform that serves to fuse both areas. This endeavour is further enhanced by black timber elements (again employed in interior and exterior applications) to strengthen the connection.

3. Time spent indoors or out? Or perhaps both, at the same time? The interconnecting patio space with a window slider system that can be opened on an angle: as such, the living and kitchen are literally connected by the outside terrace.

1. The kitchen's black and white oak combo is replicated in the choice of dining furniture. Simple thinking equals simple living.

2–3. White oak panels add decorative appeal *and* practicality. Smart storage is key to successful small-space living.

space "breathes," the simple material roster forging an alliance that plays boldly with the perception of space.

Integrated cabinets accentuate the interior's graphic feel and, as well as being literally beautiful, conceal the TV set when not in use. Further visual trickery is served via the black wood stove that appears to disappear, set against a dark-toned backdrop. You can "taste" the planning in this cabin. It's just so damned tailored...

Employing both dark and light notes across one elevation, the kitchen's skin is split down a seam, a bold statement that creates a split personality and a cool talking point that, once again, distracts from literal proportions to confuse spatial perception. Just keep thinking that this entire cabin measures less than 600 sf (56 sqm). It's a triumph, huh?

And of course, when proportions are restricted, smart space-saving solutions are called for. In this context, underfloor heating, generous ceiling heights and acres of tailored storage keep the rooms (and the minds of visitors) free of discernable

clutter. Yes, it's diminutive, but it punches above its weight in terms of atmosphere and overall experience.

In every sense, this precisely tailored cabin is a model example of a "tiny house." It's smart and comfortable, but with no concessions to quality in either its architectural or interior design. Couple all that with amazing exposure to the outdoors, and this respite's takeaway is clear: as much as "the bigger the better" maxim is relevant in certain contexts, "the *smaller* the better" rejoinder is justifiably relevant. As long, that is, as one's outlook remains vast. Yup, even with small spectacles, you can still see the world.

1. Stairway to heaven—the painted white stair and stairwell pick up the glow of light from the upstairs window to create a cleansing, heavenly ascent.

2. In an integrated wall of bedroom storage, it makes sense to break up the expanse with an open dressing-table surface or home office.

3. Full-height oak cabinets offer bedside function and wardrobe space, the twin functions (from one element) essentially simplifying proceedings.

Offering luxury and sanctuary, this haven in the forest seems to float above the ground as the vertical-timber supporting structure blends into the surrounding slender trees.

The Treehouse

LOCATION
Durham, Ontario, Canada

COMPLETION YEAR (FOR RENOVATION)
2010

OWNERS
Michael and Lynne Knowlton

ARCHITECTS
Michael and Lynne Knowlton, in association with Nathan Buhler, BLDG Workshop

INTERIOR DESIGNER
Lynne Knowlton

CONTRACTOR
Various

SIZE
200 sf (16 sqm) (tree house);
185 sf (17 sqm) (cabin)

NOTABLE BUILDING MATERIALS
Cedar, oak and pine (much of which is reclaimed or salvaged) with steel insertions, where required, to augment structural integrity; structure is set under a shingle roof

UTILITIES
Electricity, heating and water (on-grid supply), with well water in ancillary guest cabin and washroom; waste (septic system)

PHOTOGRAPHY
Lynne Knowlton

Every so often we stumble across a property so sublimely gorgeous, we swoon. Which is precisely what happened when first we visited the tree-house cabin retreat of visionary Lynne Knowlton and her husband Michael.

The tiny, elevated structure sits within the limbs of a densely wooded copse, which means that during summer months—when leaf coverage is verdant—the achingly cool nest is partially shielded from view, cosseted by thick foliage. When fall arrives, however, and Mother Nature sheds her plumage, the tiny domain is gradually revealed, in all its rustic glory. And it's a breathtaking affair.

The couple bought the land upon which their tree house sits some eighteen years past and it was, in fact, in the property's farmhouse that they raised their children. Several years later,

when a fierce tornado ripped through the county, essentially destroying a neighbour's barn, Lynne was offered the savable wood, and jumped at the chance to repurpose it into an asset her family could properly enjoy.

Lynne, you see, had long harboured a dream to build for her children a tree house, and it would be with the generously gifted lumber that she and Michael would realize that ambition. And so it came to pass that, whenever the busy couple's diary could be squeezed of a little free time, a modest structure was birthed, on naive lumber posts, within the cradle of the tall trees that overlooked the family farmhouse.

The children loved it, as did their friends, and it soon became a gathering point for local kids who relished the opportunity to play in the quirky, elevated nest. What, after all, wasn't to love? Haven't we all, at some point in our lives, dreamed of escaping to such an idyllic spot? To a haven perched high above the world, safely away from the stresses of modern-day life?

1–2. As a tree house, particularly in the commercial oeuvre, it would have been difficult to provide facilities for meal preparation and washing. To this end, rather than shoehorn in function where space, or indeed health and safety requirements, don't allow, a bathroom wing at ground level provides every modern convenience, whilst cooking facilities (and another bedroom nook) are located in the secondary cabin that sits to the side of the main tree house.

2

But, of course, time passes and children grow, and the appeal of the tree house—to the Knowlton kids and their pals, certainly, began to wane. However, all was not lost: a new opportunity for the previous play zone would soon emerge, thanks to its visionary's ambitious and unstoppable creativity.

Ah, yes, perchance to dream. Given that Lynne regularly stole away to the tree-top nest (it is, after all, just a short walk from the farmhouse) to curl up with a good book and a coffee, she began to reappraise the structure. It was simply too beautiful, too atmospheric, to leave undercapitalized. There had to be a new opportunity, in some shape or form.

Might there be potential commercial worth to the space? Could it be transformed into a sweet little holiday rental? She whispered the plans to her social circle, all of whom thought it was a great idea (as did the parents of her children's friends) so, without further ado, she set to work envisioning its conversion and extension.

But of course little, these days, is easy. As the tree house's purpose was potentially changing—from private kids' den to public space—a host of alterations had to be made to satisfy township regulations and building guidelines. To meet safety requirements, for instance, the structural piers had to be strengthened and the ladder access morphed into a staircase (with a rigid banister), whilst operable windows and doors were required to replace the previous (altogether more temporary) insertions which had been added on an ad-hoc basis over the years.

And so, across multiple meetings with planners, Lynne remained focused, her ambition for the beautiful structure gaining momentum every day. She imagined precisely how it might feel. She considered the way in which one area would yield to the next. And she dreamed of the joy it would bring to others, as indeed it had done to her own family.

Together with her husband and children's help, the Treehouse, Mark Two, eventually emerged: every bit as beautiful as the original iteration, but now ready for a whole new market to enjoy.

1. Shouldn't every tree house have a brightly coloured slide to provide easy descent? When a nearby children's playhouse was being decommissioned, Lynne claimed an old slide that was destined for landfill. Carefully and securely attached to the structure, it provides a fun extra dimension that guests are guaranteed to remember.

2–3. A large proportion of construction materials and many of the furnishings that pepper the tree house interior were auction finds, salvage items, or pieces bought from consignment stores. After stripping paint to reveal the natural wood grain, or painted to provide contrast, they were carefully arranged throughout to create a lived-in, time-worn aesthetic.

4. When confines are tight, learn to examine creative ways to make your space come alive. If you don't have a dining room (or need to augment living space), for example, do as Lynne did and take it outdoors. The underside of the tree house is arranged as an ideal spot for alfresco eating, and a space in which to lounge in hammocks or swing chairs on balmy evenings.

A secondary living area and a dramatically appointed jet-toned cabana kitchen are set to the side of the tree house and cabin, whilst, in the walls of an old barn, a swimming pool was recently added to take advantage of Canada's warmer months.

The beautiful retreat, it's safe to report, provides visitors with an overwhelming sense of joy. First family came, then friends visited … and then, when word spread, requests poured in from online rental agencies and paying guests. Today, it's regarded as one of the world's most popular tree-house destinations.

Due to limited floor space, it makes sense to consider vertical opportunity. In this regard, the mezzanine bedroom—accessed by a sturdy ladder—provides ample space for sleeping, whilst serving as a comfortable retreat for reading or daydreaming. Overall, the tree house might not be huge, but clever zoning has given its every square inch valuable purpose.

Lynne's project, for example, boasts a perfect little seating nook, an attractive balcony upon which to lounge in age-worn leather armchairs whilst surveying the softly undulating countryside, and a sweet little area in which to prepare drinks and light snacks.

Form and function are carefully married to make the overall experience as comfortable as possible. Accessories and decorative

1–2. When colouration is significantly monochrome, it's important to add extra textural layers to provide depth. Failing to do this can make visuals appear somewhat one-dimensional. If your scheme is, for example, for the most part white, endeavour to add various snowy shades, each of which should proffer a different tactile quality. Think, for instance, about painted wood, natural lumber, rough linens and smooth cottons. When adding visual texture, it really is a case of the more the merrier.

3. Painting in a predominantly white palette ensures proportions feel as generous as possible. The most important note is *contrast*, which in this case is successfully telegraphed via multiple wood finishes, subtle colour pops and generous natural wood detailing.

4. The most successful retreats blur the lines between indoors and out. Lynne enhances this balance by framing the vista with simple furniture and accessories.

layers feel lovingly chosen and carefully curated. Wooden surfaces are exactingly sanded so as to be perfectly smooth as excited hands navigate the space. And linens, textiles and cushions are immaculately groomed to provide everyone who visits with that "first-time" feeling.

The secret to the respite's success? Well, as we see it, Lynne's aesthetic feels simultaneously new and old, if that's not a contradiction in terms. Nothing seems forced; it all feels like it came together organically, over time. Each artifact, each layer, each item carefully chosen to become a jigsaw-puzzle piece, building the bigger picture. It's therefore a credit, at all times, to its visionary, Lynne . . .

Sharply executed and, literally, straight to the point: the cabin's angled facade is absolutely stunning.

Villa Vingt

LOCATION	SIZE
Lac-Beauport, Quebec, Canada	3,444 sf (320 sqm)
COMPLETION YEAR	**NOTABLE BUILDING MATERIALS**
2017	Wood frame set on a concrete foundation, steel stairs, concrete feature walls
OWNERS	
Clients of Bourgeois/ Lechasseur Architects	**UTILITIES**
	On-grid supply
ARCHITECT	
Bourgeois/Lechasseur Architects	**PHOTOGRAPHY**
	Adrien Williams
CONTRACTOR	
Vent du Sud	

It's astonishing to consider the transition that concrete has made in the estimations of designers and architects the world over. For the longest time, concrete was perceived simply as a structural medium and poured, typically, to form exterior walls in apartments and condos. For the most part, concrete was deigned to strengthen the environments throughout which it was employed, but it was hidden from sight by subsequent layers and finishing.

This observed, there existed a minority sector of the construction industry who saw concrete in an altogether different light. At the more adventurous end of home building, concrete was used to add an unexpected edge and was seen by certain—perhaps more daring—architects and visionaries as an exciting medium with which to add "anti-style" statements.

When, in the 1920s, emerging Bauhausian architects began to use it to build quickly, concrete was deemed, by many onlookers, as cold, stark and sterile. And when Brutalism entered the

fray in the 1950s, pouring concrete scorn over traditional "tame" building aesthetics, many commentators scoffed at the typically stark (but in our opinion oft' beautiful) edifices that typified its vernacular.

Lately, and perhaps more than ever before, concrete has ventured out of the dark and into the light. It's fair to report the building medium is having a moment, and about that we are little short of thrilled. In urban and suburban construction, concrete is fast becoming a visible finish of choice, a fashion-forward material for developers and homeowners alike to infuse their environments with a little hard-edged cool.

We, too, have fallen under the spell of concrete. Little wonder, then, that when we spotted Villa Vingt, we fell in love. Anchored as it is on a sloping site next to the Le Relais ski resort in Lac-Beauport, the holiday retreat is a commanding affair, with vast planes of visible concrete displayed at every turn.

Level one acts as a base that leans against the angled ground and opens up completely to the north. It's a feast of architectural drama, with the upper floor appearing to hover above the concrete ground floor. The living areas are expertly cantilevered—and,

1. The lower-level garage swallows up vehicles like a Bond villain's lair: at once beautiful and practical, and a smart way to store cars without consuming real estate above ground.

2. The cantilever projecting from the structure's front elevation appears to float into infinity.

through maximized fenestration, unobstructed, painting-like views of the surrounding mountain landscape can be witnessed.

To help the program make economic sense (and to facilitate an easier transition through planning), the original basement configuration remained. "One of the most significant challenges of this build," explains Olivier Bourgeois, of the architectural practice Bourgeois/Lechasseur, "was working with the original foundations of the house that already existed on the site. That said, these considerations made sense in the long run. To observe how the house has transitioned, while working around a little of its original sensibility, is actually very satisfying."

It's an undeniably fascinating house, with an abundance of shapes and structural outlines that proffer an alluring, albeit modernistic, envelope. Planning a project like this, of course, requires careful dialogue with several parties to ensure the very best results. Bourgeois explains that it was necessary to mix and interplay materials to create these geometric outlines. "We used a combination of large-scale wooden beams, for example, and massive steel supports, to achieve the cantilever and the large openings. Working with a competent practice of structural

engineers allowed us, as a collective, to ensure everything was properly considered and finely tuned."

As we see it, the talented architect's pride is more than warranted. It's fair to say that this home—and its facade's striking horizontality—create a strong presence in the panorama. From the moment of approach, the richness of the upper-floor white cedar ceilings, viewable from outside, capture attention. The warm material continues under the roofline to reinforce the transition from inside to out. Everything appears so beautifully planned, which of course it is.

We ask Bourgeois which aspects of the design he thinks could most easily be transferred, as inspiration, to the projects of those who fall in love with the cabin, and he's swift on the uptake. "Optimize the scale of windows to welcome in light and allow views to be enjoyed at their best," he answers. "And I always say that projecting roof lines, as much as possible, is a reliable way to add presence while limiting the invasion of sun."

Internally, the mood is precisely considered, almost geometrical, the resultant aesthetic playing well to the homeowners'

1. Whilst admittedly urban in its aesthetic, the room's pared-back nature and striking window formations allow visitors to focus on the surrounding landscape.

2. As viewed from the sunken sitting area, the fireplace elevation and kitchen diner appear to be on stage, a perfect setting for the performance of everyday life.

3–4. The mix of painted and natural wood finishes delivers a perfect recipe, and beautiful contrast, in this geometrically precise kitchen.

1. Concrete and steel are no longer the preserve of the elite home-building fraternity, and neither are they deemed "cold" or "unfriendly." In fact, they're considered part of the "new luxury" language of architecture.

2–3. A staircase that's a veritable work of art. The precision craftsmanship of steel on concrete makes a triumphant statement in this starkly beautiful retreat.

modernist sensibilities. And there are surprises, everywhere. The dining room's zenithal skylight, for example, proffers an unexpected view of the treetops, its insertion allowing indirect light to play on elements of the interior such as the cedar slats. The window also serves as a useful light source to further brighten the interior as the sun passes over the building.

There's actually so much to enjoy whilst viewing this home from home. The central concrete wall, for example, gives the project a sense of sustained verticality, and its textural detail (a result of "embracing" the rough finish left by the formwork) adds visual and tactile interest. The staircase (which sits to the side of the concrete wall) layers schematic richness through the duality of the surrounding materials, namely concrete and steel.

We can more than imagine ourselves vacationing here. Secretly, that's how we evaluate a lot of the cabins and retreats we visit. If we have a sense we could check in, unpack our bags and get into the spirit of a place, we feel an immediately bigger connection. As indeed we do with this respite. It's a spirited home, and we'd be perfectly comfortable here with a few stolen moments to unwind.

The cabin's exterior is thoroughly underplayed, fashioned from graphite-toned metal which contrasts perfectly with the natural and ever-changing surroundings: grey and green in spring and summer, grey and amber in autumn, and grey and white in deepest winter.

Vipp Shelter

LOCATION
Lake Immeln, Sweden

SIZE
592 sf (55 sqm)

COMPLETION YEAR
2014

NOTABLE BUILDING MATERIALS
Steel and glass

OWNER
Vipp

UTILITIES
On-grid supply

ARCHITECT
Vipp

PHOTOGRAPHY
Anders Hviid-Haglund

CONTRACTORS
A collaboration between
Vipp, Velux Commercial
and panoramah!

Vipp's love affair with steel can be charted as far back as 1939, when Holger Nielsen, a young Danish metalworker, crafted a sturdy, pedal-controlled bin for use in his wife Marie's hair salon. Seventy years later, the pedal bin is celebrated not just in Denmark, but around the world, as a functional design icon—an observation, as we see it, of function and style paired in perfect harmony. In 2009, the ubiquitous bin became part of the permanent design collection at MoMA in New York, accreditation that further elevated its status, this time to veritable design deity.

Today, still family-driven and family-owned, Vipp has grown to encompass a large portfolio of industrial design products, each of which has been developed with the same functional philosophy as the pedal bin. From laundry baskets to steel kitchens, from coffee tables to daybeds, Vipp brand values have been realized through many exciting mediums across the last decades.

One such expression is the Vipp Shelter, a truly magical forest retreat nestled at the side of a quiet lake in Skåne County,

Sweden. The shelter is considered part of the Vipp Hotel, a hostelry with a distinct difference to others. Instead of many rooms in one location, Vipp offers unique rooms at various destinations across different locations in Copenhagen, including a unique loft and the Chimney House.

The "hotel" rooms are designed to provide a uniquely unforgettable experience, and, because they're all single dwellings, guests enjoy total privacy at every turn. As the brand says: "As soon as you check in at the Vipp Hotel, it's effectively fully booked…"

Examining the structure's design reveals Vipp's ethos: utter dependability and utter lack, therein, of any type of fuss. In this property, steel is a recurring element, one which cuts through the shelter's frame and facade, appearing again in the utilitarian but beautiful kitchen cabinetry modules, and even its accessories.

Favouring a "less is more" attitude, items have been incorporated based on need as opposed to want, with each piece perfectly aligned with its surroundings. In reality, it's the "family

1. Time to reflect—the glass and steel structure glistens, like a jewel, in the sunlight.

2. The kitchen, dining space and living area conspire to create a free-flowing template, with sliding glass walls taking the notion of open-concept to a new level: visitors can become entirely immersed in nature, climate permitting.

3. Positioning is paramount—the Vipp shelter offers amazing vistas across the lake, whilst sheltered in the trees to protect against direct sunlight and harsh winds. Even in a steel box, nature can still be your protector.

The kitchen features a large island packed with storage compartments and all manner of life-enhancing modern inclusions. The cabin, and its dark metal furniture detail, minimize "visual" disturbance. As such, courtesy of the simple vision, the only observable elements are dark metal and nature.

resemblance" shared by the building and its contents that suffuses the project's overall identity with precise cohesion.

Tranquility, as we see it, is the luxury that flows, in abundance, from lake and sky views that far exceed any typical star rating. Immersion in nature is the raison d'être; the ubiquitous hotel TV set replaced by huge windows that offer occupants a widescreen to nature.

As far as functionality is concerned, food-prep quarters are specifically designed for slow living—the equipped Vipp kitchen affording guests the opportunity to set a languid mood whilst preparing meals. Meals which can then be enjoyed by a roaring fire: thanks to the shelter's open-concept nature, the kitchen, technically, has its own hearth.

It's hard not to appreciate the beautiful structure, not least its moody, jet-toned shell. Black, in the design context, works so well for us: it's sophisticated and mysterious and easily imports schematic drama. In the Vipp Shelter, we love the way the smart interior and restrained layering further elevate the project.

2. The shelter features concrete floors with built-in radiant heating, but a wood-burning stove provides extra warmth—and soothing, flickering light—as required. And, of course, it offers the primitive satisfaction of gathering wood to start a fire, rather than simply flicking a switch.

3. Room service—the table and chairs, whilst intended for dining, can be easily deployed as a convenient workstation.

4. In the kitchen, beauty and functionality combine in the shape of crockery and glassware that remain close at hand, where they're most needed.

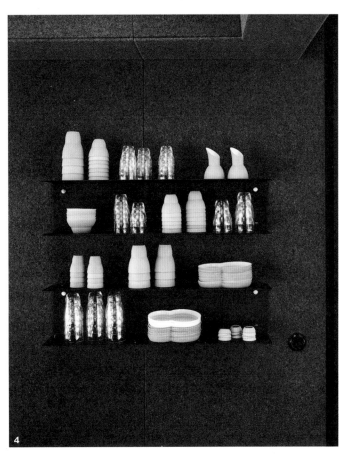

And we love the way the large glazing panels appear to recede as they frame the landscape, allowing the rich forestation, the sky and the twinkling lake to shine and be appreciated in all their brilliant glory.

In the loft, accessed by a wide ebony ladder, the sky really is the limit: the elevated pod boasts a glass ceiling so guests can sleep under the stars, bathed in the night sky, and awaken sheltered in a dewy forest canopy. "We craved birdsong and open skies," says Morten Bo Jensen, chief designer on the project. "The shelter is a result of the dream to get out of the city with just necessities and nothing more. Tranquility designed as a large-scale Vipp product."

Most of us are by now familiar with "forest bathing," a term which derives from the Japanese *shinrin-yoku*, meaning to take in the "healing" atmosphere of the forest. But this special space goes beyond bathing and into the realms of deep diving—buoyed, at all times, in the verdant arms of Mother Nature.

For all the shelter's straight lines and contemporary styling, it sits remarkably comfortably in the forest. In actual fact it's

1. The roof extension houses a comfortable yet compact sleeping loft, with ceiling skylights that allow occupants to sleep under the stars and awaken with the morning sun. Go on: leave your watch behind and let nature be your timekeeper.

2. A steel ladder, a fun and modern way by which to climb into bed, leads the way to the upper sleeping area.

3. The shower room features the iconic steel bin, the very item that birthed the Vipp empire so long ago. It's a nod to the past, served up perfectly in Vipp's vision for the future.

4. A daybed details the main floor, creating an increased sense of comfort that's ideal for one—or even better, two—to snuggle up with by day or, indeed, night.

super welcoming and friendly, traits that most onlookers might not automatically associate with a 592-sf (55-sqm) steel object that weighs a whopping twenty-five tons. The structure, however, challenges those perceptions with man-made and natural elements combining to create an intimate, cosseting experience.

Why does it work so well? The strength of the shelter's steel skeleton provides protection, whilst the glass-panelled "skin" lays bare its inhabitants. It's that juxtaposition of protection and exposure that challenges the senses, thereby encouraging occupants to "feel" their surroundings and get closer to nature.

Jensen, we learned, conceived the Vipp Shelter as a product, rather than a piece of architecture—one that's capable of fusing perfectly with its surroundings, wherever they may be. The starting point wasn't a piece of land from which he felt compelled to draw inspiration: he actually wanted to create a product that could go anywhere. "There's plenty of amazing architecture out there," he suggests, "but we wanted something different, an escape in the form of an object designed down to last detail, where the only choice left to the customer is where to put it."

1. The seasons may change, but the Vipp Shelter hotel remains as a beacon of health, happiness and hospitality.

So from where, precisely, does his design inspiration originate? "Large-volume objects like planes or ferries. They're clear references in the design. Just like these products, the shelter is a voluminous, transportable, design construction."

Taking this contained approach to space planning works well in compact-home, condominium, or shipping-container architecture: anywhere where proportions are tight. Essentially it all comes down to making every inch of space "deliver," in terms of form and function. Think about how much property costs—do you want to waste even an inch of what you've got? For that which you've paid? Precisely.

In the twenty-first-century world, technology abounds with apps and devices designed to control our surroundings. In the forest, the Vipp Shelter takes a pared-down, easy-living approach to function that embodies the essence of a vacation retreat.

"If you're cold," explains Jensen, "you simply heat up the shelter's centrally positioned fireplace for an equal distribution of heat. And if you're warm, just slide open the parallel windows to

2. Composite social functions are nicely spread across the main floor, and especially appreciable as viewed from outside when darkness falls.

create natural air conditioning." His are simple observations, but they make so much sense. "By locating the house in the deep deciduous woods, we're able to take advantage of the leaves as shading during summer. In winter, when the trees lose their leaves, the building's black exterior absorbs sunlight, so for the fireplace, there's a reduction in fuel consumption." To suggest that the Vipp Shelter is well planned is an understatement. It's meticulously well considered.

Via his "product design" approach, Jensen and his team have delivered a "hotel" like no other. Okay, so there's no room service, no pool, no valet parking and no pay-per-view TV. But the shelter's scientific simplicity and attention to detail more than make up for that, delivering a new brand of luxury and a chance to recharge and commune—in a sublimely uncomplicated manner—with nature. In terms of star rating, this escape slays the five-star experience. Who, after all, needs a butler, when the Vipp Shelter and its friendly forest cater, perfectly, to every conceivable need?

A traditional log cabin has been updated by changing the colour of the logs from dark varnish to a muted, blue-grey finish and by adding smooth Peregrine limestone pavers and rusted corten steel to provide definition.

Yellow Bell

LOCATION
Jackson, Wyoming, USA

COMPLETION YEAR
2015

OWNERS
Clients of CLB Architects

ARCHITECT
CLB Architects

INTERIOR DESIGNER
CLB Architects

CONTRACTORS
Tennyson Ankeny
Construction, Kelsey
Woodworks (carpentry)

SIZE
4,612 sf (428 sqm)

NOTABLE BUILDING MATERIALS
Log and plaster walls,
Douglas fir floors, limestone
pavers

UTILITIES
On-grid supply with forced
air, auxiliary radiant and a gas
fireplace for heating

PHOTOGRAPHY
Audrey Hall

For a certain contingent of cabin owners, timber finishes are the be-all and end-all, with wood, in its various forms, left exposed—nay, embraced—at every turn. For these people, timber is sacrosanct—a medium to be revealed, celebrated, and not, under *any* circumstances, painted.

Wood, as a building component, is seldom more visible than when used in the construction of log cabins. With those, it really is a case of (if we may turn a popular maxim on its head) what you get is what you see.

And we see a lot of them in our travels. The log cabin, by its very nature, is a quintessentially North American affair—the poster child for those who want to follow in the footsteps of America's first European settlers, to live in homes that feel like they were literally born of the forest.

Just like the timber from which they're constructed, log cabins are, for so many onlookers, a subject of reverence. So

1. The comfortable living room is the perfect home for the owners' antique Japanese tansu chest, and for the striking horse-racing painting purchased from a California antique store. The blue top strip shows the painting's original patina (previously protected by a frame) before the passage of time discoloured the painting.

2. The Kravet fabric sofa is positioned to enjoy the fireplace and views to the Tetons beyond. This room is a real textural feast—the sofa, carpet, throws and cushions (and even the artwork) contribute to the layering that makes the space effortlessly comfortable.

3. The flat, drywalled sections simplify the surface and, in doing so, allow the gallery of artworks to be displayed.

imagine the raised eyebrows were anyone to take the reins of a rustic log home with the intention of transforming it into a white-painted, twenty-first-century world, a space that would eventually become equal parts personal art gallery and striking, contemporary abode.

Well, that's precisely what happened when an artist couple, in tight collaboration with CLB Architects, purchased and transformed this formerly dowdy retreat into a bright, welcoming environment that boasts an effortless connection between indoors and out. Managing a complex mix of renovation, preservation and personalization, however, didn't come without an attendant précis of controversial design decisions.

A fireplace was removed, sections of logs were faced with drywall, and timber, everywhere, was painted white. But oh, the finished product: a gallery-style space that speaks for itself as a wildly inviting retreat. And a space that wholly represents its owners, whilst retaining many of the characteristics—and rustic charm—of the past.

The project's "rehabilitation" began by gutting the oppressively dark master bedroom suite. Throughout the cabin, several wood elevations were drywalled to create lighting channels and to serve as flat wall space for the owner's extensive art collection, with alabaster-tinted lacquer applied thereafter, to brighten and unify new and existing surfaces.

The original wide-plank Douglas fir floors were retained and re-finished to a smooth, ebony appearance that contrasts the white walls to undeniably dramatic effect. The trick to approaching a build like this is maximizing the best of what already exists, whilst being simultaneously brave enough to eliminate elements (compliant, of course, with planning and consents) that no longer work.

Other changes included installing a partial wall between the dining area and kitchen to create a sense of separation (without entirely obliterating the zone's open-concept integrity) and the reengineering—and strengthening—of an office wall in order to install a large, transformative window. The resultant glass

1. The snowy-toned floor and wall tiles continue the white story and deliver a feeling of purity and cleanliness. Essential elements in any relaxing environment.

2. A mountain of relaxation—a floor-to-ceiling bathroom window frames the Grand Tetons, whilst flooding the room with natural light. The stools were log ends (sawn off during the reno) which the cabin owners fashioned into a simple trio.

3. Simplicity and elegance—the guest bedroom balances painted timber and wood to create a forest of calm. The wheels on the bed are a nice nod to industrial style.

1, 3. Even the kitchen has galleryspace surfaces. Meanwhile, walls and shelves showcase the owners' art collection.

2. The hound and the head-line—artwork choices are at once playful and provoc- ative. A large canine figure offers welcome against the backdrop of an installation of newspapers collected by the homeowner during the 2003 U.S. invasion of Iraq.

portal provides an amazing wake-up each morning, situated as it is at the foot of the bed to embrace the beautiful Grand Teton view.

When it came time to tackle the cabin's exterior, the hefty log inventory was blasted to remove years of sun-damaged varnish. This done, a muted blue-grey finish, picking up tones from the limestone pavers that carry from the interior to the exterior, was applied to straddle the line between rustic retreat and the interior's gallery-like reversion.

The cabin's approach is framed with trees, lazy grasses and modern hardscaping, the combination of which is at once sculptural and welcoming. Landscape planners Hershberger Design used rusted corten steel partitions to screen the driveway from the house, defining the walkway, thereafter, with Peregrine limestone to suffuse the scene with precision modernity.

1. Peregrine limestone pavers serve as smooth modern contrast to the log structure's blue-grey appearance.

2. The approach to the property is framed with trees, lazy grasses and modern hardscaping to create a tailored but distinctly natural feel.

3. Landscape visionaries Hershberger Design used rusted corten steel partitions to screen and provide definition to the driveway.

The idea of employing "weathering" steel (that's architectural parlance for rusted metal) complements the cabin's rustic heritage whilst updating the garden approach through sheer steely definition. It's fair to suggest that an application such as this is one the few occasions in life when rust is an ally.

To properly appraise the interior, as we see it, is to observe a final vision of unique personality: the connection to the outside is tangible in every room, and the owner's art, displayed throughout, takes pride of place in what's undoubtedly a very livable—and indeed lovable—gallery.

The renovation program, which saw the cabin transform from its formerly dark, dated iteration into a contemporary rustic retreat for the future, is breathtaking. And, of course, testament to the idea that any building can be transitioned to become a platform where its occupants can be their very, very best selves. Now isn't that exactly what every escape should deliver?

Directory

The architects, designers, builders and clever people featured here.

ACKNOWLEDGEMENTS

This book is dedicated, in loving memory, to our parents, Trudy and Robert McAllister and Claire and Daniel Ryan.

Our grateful thanks to the roster of gifted architects, designers and photographers whose beautiful work features across the pages of this book. Without their vision, skill sets and resources, writing *Escapology* would have been impossible. We also extend our gratitude to our featured cabin owners for generously opening their doors. It has been our pleasure to research and showcase these incredible abodes.

To the wonderful team at Figure 1 Publishing—thanks to Michelle Meade, Jessica Sullivan, Chris Labonté and Lara Smith.

To Sundance, Meghan and the team at The Spotlight Agency in Toronto, to the gang at Cottage Life where our TV shows *Colin and Justin's Cabin Pressure* and *Great Canadian Cottages* air, and to our *Cityline* family for their support since we landed in Canada some fourteen years past. To our literary agent Hilary McMahon, thank you for steering this journey.

To Anna, Deborah, Joey, Nicole, Mark and the wonderfully creative team at TJX Canada, where, via stores like Homesense, Winners and Marshalls, the Colin+Justin Home collection is available.

To our editor Martin Slofstra and the team at the *Toronto Sun*/Postmedia. To the wildly creative Ann Banks, the irrepressible Sue Watson and the endlessly patient Amanda Lowe, and to all those with whom we worked (and by whom we were nurtured) at BBC Birmingham where our wee journey began, some two decades past.

To our families in Britain for keeping the home fires burning.

To our very dear friends Michaela and Norm Davies. We cherish every moment we spend together. Thank you for being, on so many occasions, our Canadian family, and our voices of reason.

To Fhiona Mackay, the Pontes (Elaine, George, Tallulah and Jasmine), Debby McGregor, Alyzen Thyne, Nina and Greg Deakin, Carol and Lewis Tritschler, Mark Aldridge and Mark Hooper.

To Chris and Susan, and all our pals on Drag Lake. To Catriona, Paolo and family, to Lady Di and the Mitchells and to Tim and Noelle.

To Cheryl Torrenueva, Michael Rosas and precious Reyna for enduring friendship, endless fun, and shared loud laughter!

And to the unstintingly creative Bob Newnham (whose friendly counsel we never take for granted) and the entire gang at Sunspace Sunrooms, for stellar support and equally stellar product!

And finally, thank you to Beamer and Brutus Small for unstinting feline loyalty as we composed this body of work.

THE AUTHORS

Scottish-born Colin and Justin have been designing homes for the last twenty-five years in the UK, France, Spain, Canada and Australia. They have featured in countless newspapers and magazines including the *Globe and Mail, The Times, The Telegraph, Grand Designs Australia, Livingetc* and *Dwell*.

They have hosted numerous shows on BBC UK, Channel 5 UK, ITV UK, HGTV Canada and the Cottage Life network. They appear frequently on the Canadian lifestyle show *Cityline*, which also airs in the U.S. on CBS's DABL network.

The "Colin+Justin Home" home product range is available in the UK, Canada, Australia and the U.S.

Colin and Justin flipped their first house thirty years ago and have flipped nearly twenty city homes since. Eight years ago, they dipped their toes into the world of country real estate by renovating a Canadian log cabin. They soon became hooked on the rural idyll, and there started a love affair with the great outdoors that, thus far, has seen them transform five down-at-heel cabins into luxurious lakeside retreats.